Title: *Stories & Heart*

Author: Sharon Price John

ISBN: 978-1-95086-344-0

Price: $27.99

Pages: 272

This is an Author Review Copy for the purpose of editorial review only and not for distribution.

Praise for *Stories & Heart*

Having known Sharon when she worked her first job in advertising, it was an honor to read about her incredible journey to CEO. Along with her engaging stories of success, failures, and challenges, Sharon provides thought-provoking lessons for life and for business.

—DEE HASLAM
CEO of Haslam Sports
Owner of the Cleveland Browns

This book is exceptional and will be meaningful to anyone who wants to open themselves up to be all they can be!

—JILL BARAD
Former CEO of Mattel

Having experienced the power of Sharon's leadership firsthand, she brings her signature style of humanity, creativity, intelligence, and humor to this powerful memoir of her life and career. In this book, Sharon gives what she naturally gives to anyone who meets her: The tools and techniques to see, design, and create your best future. Sharon inspires you with her own vulnerability and ability to drive extraordinary results.

—SARAH PERSONETTE
Chief Consumer Officer of Twitter

As one of America's most admired presidents and CEOs of a publicly traded company, Sharon Price John shares her life experiences through themes and storytelling while including thought-provoking questions for readers along the way. Sharon's vast experiences along with her strong intuition are her superpowers! This is a must-read! Entertaining, personal, and a great read on success.

—STEVE SCHUSSLER
Author of the national best seller It's a Jungle in There; *Creator of Rainforest Café, T-Rex, Yak and Yeti, and The Boathouse, all at Disney World in Orlando, Florida*

I found *Stories & Heart* absolutely fabulous! I want to read it again and again. The advice is perfect! As the Build-A-Bear franchisee for Australia, I really enjoy working with Sharon and appreciate her ability to lead the company to success in such tough times. I found this story of her life truly inspiring. I highly recommend *Stories & Heart*. It will be helpful to every reader, because the sound advice is highly practical. We all want to live a "life that we love," but very few manage to do so. Sharon has found a wonderful way to positively impact the lives of others.

—NORMA ROSENHAIN
Founder and CEO of Creata

Stories & Heart brings life to those everyday moments that create who we are and who we will become. By providing a peek into how she has used her experiences as lessons to help identify her purpose, Sharon inspires us to make use of our individual journeys. I'm reminded that there are no detours in life, just experiences of great possibility, and that when you have an open heart and embrace these moments you can bring life to the dreams you didn't know you had. She gives us inspiration, a reminder to be brave and bold, and has even included interactive prompts to help claim that unique power inside each of us. I absolutely loved this book, and have written aspirational notes and reminders to myself on every page. I can't wait to experience it all unfold.

—LYSA RATLIFF
Head of KABOOM!

Stories & Heart not only reaches inside to explore what really creates a successful, fulfilling career and life, but Sharon John gives you a compass of the heart. John is a pioneer and a woman who has never met a challenge she did not suit up for.

—TENA CLARK
Founder and CEO of DMI Music
Composer/Producer, Speaker, Activist

ST♥RIES
& HEART

SHARON PRICE JOHN

CEO OF BUILD-A-BEAR WORKSHOP

ST♥RIES
& HEART

UNLOCK THE POWER OF PERSONAL STORIES
to create a life you love

ForbesBooks

Published by ForbesBooks, Charleston, South Carolina.
Member of Advantage Media Group.

ForbesBooks is a registered trademark, and the ForbesBooks colophon is a trademark of Forbes Media, LLC.

Printed in the United States of America.

10 9 8 7 6 5 4 3 2 1

ISBN: 978-1-950863-44-0
LCCN: 2022900439

This custom publication is intended to provide accurate information and the opinions of the author in regard to the subject matter covered. It is sold with the understanding that the publisher, Advantage|ForbesBooks, is not engaged in rendering legal, financial, or professional services of any kind. If legal advice or other expert assistance is required, the reader is advised to seek the services of a competent professional.

 Advantage Media Group is proud to be a part of the Tree Neutral® program. Tree Neutral offsets the number of trees consumed in the production and printing of this book by taking proactive steps such as planting trees in direct proportion to the number of trees used to print books. To learn more about Tree Neutral, please visit **www.treeneutral.com**.

Since 1917, Forbes has remained steadfast in its mission to serve as the defining voice of entrepreneurial capitalism. ForbesBooks, launched in 2016 through a partnership with Advantage Media Group, furthers that aim by helping business and thought leaders bring their stories, passion, and knowledge to the forefront in custom books. Opinions expressed by ForbesBooks authors are their own. To be considered for publication, please visit **www.forbesbooks.com**.

This book is dedicated to you and the sincere hope that you'll embrace the wonderful journey of creating a life you love.

Why wouldn't you?

CONTENTS

INTRODUCTION

When Forbes approached me about this project, I was concerned that they were envisioning that I write a traditional business book, more typically expected of a publicly traded company CEO. But this is not a book about business. This is a book of stories. Sure, a lot of the stories are grounded in events from my career that have led to insights concerning business. But most of the stories are more personal, even from childhood, where I gleaned other valuable lessons. Even though the stories form a loose chronological arc of my life, this is not an autobiography. In fact, it is not even intended to be *about* me.

Each chapter of the book has a theme and a story followed by a "Question from the Heart," related to the narrative for you to contemplate. Next is a prompt for you to "Create Your Own Story," with an exercise reflective of the chapter theme designed to help unlock your own power of story to create a life you love.

By exploring common themes like having dreams, mustering courage, needing faith, dealing with doubt, feeling fear, enduring failure, facing loss, or making change, the goal is for this book to be as much a journey for you as it was for me. My hope is that this creates an opportunity, perhaps even a catalyst, for you to think about what really matters in your life while recognizing that the meaning you have woven around your stories not only directly impacts your own life journey but can be predictive of it. While this book is dedicated to *you*, it can only impact *you* if *you* allow it. Enjoy.

> # While this book is dedicated to *you*, it can only impact *you* if *you* allow it.

CHAPTER 1

Life's a Beech

Goals & Gumption

*The victory of success is half won when one gains the
habit of setting goals and achieving them.*
—AUGUSTINE "OG" MANDINO II

My Story

Tree climbing is not for the faint of heart. Every tree is different.
It takes planning and tenacity to scale the tough ones. Even with a
good start, you may need to change your approach to get to the most
elusive limbs. For those who have braved the climb, the reward of
seeing the world from on high is worth it. Those who haven't will
never know.

I liked climbing trees when I was little. Sometimes I would
choose a difficult one, but I also liked the occasional tall, trusty pine
with low limbs. If you can get over the annoying gummy pine tar,
they are a breeze to ascend because the branches grow parallel to the
ground, kind of like a sticky, twisting ladder to the sky.

Even now, when I see a kid in a tree or recognize the distinct smell of pine trees, I am immediately whisked back to the seventeen summers of my Tennessee childhood as much as by the aroma of blooming honeysuckle growing on the side of the old dusty barn at my grandmother's house.

My father's mother lived about ten miles outside of my small hometown, which served as the county seat of our community with its proud courthouse and surrounding square that bustled with shops and restaurants. I spent a lot of time at my grandmother's house, where both my father and grandfather were raised. It was an old white Victorian-style home that had been in our family since the 1890s. It was hugged by a generous wraparound porch with dark-green swings and featured delicate woodwork and screen doors that slammed to announce an arrival or departure. It overflowed with family stories, southern cooking, and secret places that evoked imagination. While there, I enjoyed the freedom to explore, which was commonplace for many children of that time. This unstructured play (as it is called today) was provided at my own home as well, where many of the neighborhood kids were allowed to go to the park or each other's houses without much adult supervision, as long as we followed the rules. This led to many hours outdoors occupying ourselves, especially given the lack of today's video games and cartoons on demand.

You had to leap over a minnow-filled creek that ran behind my redbrick ranch house to get to the park where we found all sorts of kid adventures. On the back side of the park, past a clearing, was a slope covered with trusty pine trees known simply as the Pine Woods. It's where we told ghost stories under the bramble, where I had my first innocent kiss, and where we slid down the packed pine needles on cardboard box remnants if someone got a new kitchen appliance, which was the closest thing to sledding some years given the rare winter snows. It was also the perfect place to climb.

I would sometimes come home marked with pine tar. My dad thought it was great to see how active I had been. Mom didn't mind either, but the house was off limits with filthy, sticky hands and pine needles in my blond ponytail. In extreme situations, she would spray me down with the hose before I could eat supper inside with the family.

Memorial Day was right around the corner, and I was looking forward to the summer school break when, between lemonade and drippy popsicles, my friends and I spent time going to the local pool, riding bikes, and climbing trees until the sun sank below the hazy orange horizon, after which we'd better get home—and fast!

But instead of enjoying our Memorial Day weekend holiday family tradition of a Saturday lake trip followed by Sunday church and placing flowers on the graves of generations of our ancestors, my dad shared some unexpected news with my big brother and me.

Our beloved grandmother had passed away in the night while sitting in her favorite chair at that old white house. It was sudden and heartbreaking. In the days to follow, I made myself sick from crying and carefully placed my childhood Bible under my pillow at night for weeks in the hope it would help me sleep. The passing of my dad's mother and our family matriarch left a hole in my heart and my life that I couldn't quite understand at the tender age of eleven. I also couldn't quite comprehend the terrible impact it had on my dad. He was close to his mom. She raised him as a single mother in the 1940s, during World War II, after his father had died in an accident when Daddy was only twelve years old. Now, he had to bury her and sell our generational homeplace in a matter of months. I witnessed my dad cry only a few times in my life, and this was one of them.

Understandably, my parents were mentally somewhere else that summer, preoccupied in the wake of the current events. So, I was left to fend for myself more than usual as the days grew warmer and longer. After the school year officially ended, I did not pack to go stay at my grandmother's house for a week or so as usual, and I did not feel like hanging out with my neighborhood friends.

Instead, I spent a lot of time walking through the park just to think, often ending up in the Pine Woods. One day, I noticed a big tree near the top of the back slope of the woods that was not a pine. Of course, it had always been there; it had just never caught my attention quite like this. It was a massive beech tree, like something out of a fairy tale. The trunk was at least the width of a tractor tire, and it had sprawling, python-like roots all around the base clinging to the incline to secure its huge body and outstretched arms.

I circled and examined it, assessing that this must be the kind of tree that had wisdom. And, boy, did I think I needed some wisdom right about then.

As far as I could tell, the biggest challenge with this tree was that the first limb was really high up, and way out of my reach. But a close second was that, unlike most trees, beech trees have smooth, silver-gray bark, which can make them more difficult to climb. I had scaled a lot of trees, but this old beech looked beyond my capabilities.

As I arched back and contemplated the large limb overhead, I could just make out what looked like initials scratched up there in the smooth bark. For sure, those bark tattoos had to be left by older kids, maybe friends of my older brother, which just made me even more determined to figure out a way to scale it. Maybe I would be the youngest kid and probably the only girl to climb it. Importantly, those carvings proved the climb was possible!

Okay, by now you may have guessed I was sometimes called a "tomboy." As early as four years old, I would tell those accusers that I was *not* a tom*boy* but a tom*girl!* Sometimes they would say, "Don't you know there's no such thing as a tom*girl?*" Dad defended me. He'd just smile and say I could be anything I wanted to be. He allowed me to be a tree climber with dirty knees and bare feet who he taught to change a tire, rewire a lamp, and back a trailer while also being perfectly fine with me having a canopy bed, hair bows, Barbies, and lots of stuffed animals. I never recall any pressure to fit into some preconceived ideal.

At the time, it was not unusual for some girls to act like they didn't know an answer in class so a boy could think he was smarter, or let a boy win a foot race even though he was slower. For a tomgirl like me, that was obviously incomprehensible.

I can't help but laugh at pictures in our family albums of me standing defiantly with my hands on my hips. I give my parents credit for trying to channel my spirit in a positive direction without dismantling it or labeling it as "bossy." I think, in an attempt to manage my temper, Daddy gave me a nickname that I did not like: Short Fuse. Best I can tell, he wanted me to learn that throwing a fit rarely helps you get what you want. He would encourage me to calm down and explain my point. Whether he knew it or not, I was learning that if I was determined with a compelling argument, I could often still achieve my objective.

This lesson was put to the test toward the end of my seventh-grade year when I overrotated a dismount on the balance beam in gymnastics practice. I fractured both the radius and ulna in my left forearm and ended up with a right-angle cast from my fingertips to my shoulder. The doctor told me it would stay on for at least six weeks. Beyond marking the end of my gymnastics competition for that season, I was incredibly upset with the whole situation because my first-ever cheerleading tryouts for the varsity junior high squad were in just a few weeks. And I had been preparing for those tryouts—literally, for *years*. The doctor wasn't sympathetic—no tryouts for me, he said.

Before you judge me about my cheerleading goal, please first consider that football and all that goes along with it is very important down south. As soon as the first crisp breeze stirs up the turning leaves, you can almost feel the excitement of the coming season opener. In my hometown the first game was usually ushered in by the weeklong county fair, where the best animals, vegetables, pies, and harness racing around were displayed. We welcomed the symbolic farewell to the humid summer as the cooler weather rekindled the eternal hope of the next football season.

People don't go to the games just because they have a son or brother playing on the team, or a daughter or sister in the band or on the cheer squad. They go because this is *their town*. Like lots of other girls, at about five or six years old, I would sit at the foot of the bleachers next to the field under the Friday-night lights to learn the cheerleading routines. So when I say I had been planning this for *years*, I'm not kidding.

Finding a way to try out against the will of my doctor with a broken arm would not be easy. Like Dad taught me, I knew I needed to be determined with a compelling argument! I made a plan to practice without permission and then do a big reveal, so they would just have to say yes!

Gymnasts are usually right-hand or left-hand tumblers. I led with my left arm, which was broken. I needed to do at least a cartwheel and a roundoff, leading with my "wrong" arm, on one hand, with the other arm in a big clunky cast—in just a couple of weeks—or I wouldn't have a snowball's chance at making the cut. After a lot of effort, I convinced my parents to let me try out by safely tumbling with one arm during a demonstration in my backyard.

I went after one of those four varsity slots with a smile on my face, hope in my heart, and a great big cast on my arm. Go Tigers! Maybe I was good, or maybe I got the sympathy vote, but I made the squad that season and for years afterward. At the time, this was a *big* moment that I believe contributed to a path of positive self-identity, but I have often wondered what made me so determined, even in the face of what looked like an impossible situation.

It seems by that point, setting goals and having gumption were clearly already part of my personality. Arguably, the tendency may have come naturally, given my "short fuse" stubbornness. But I don't believe attitudes are all about our genes. We face choices. Their outcome creates beliefs. Beliefs drive the meaning we place on events in our lives. And the meaning we attribute to things that happen can literally shape our stories and ultimately shape us.

So, what was it? Well, I think that audacious decision to try out for cheerleading with a huge cast on my arm leads right back to my beech tree Moby Dick. Every few days I privately circled the big tree in the summer of '75, strategizing, looking for a crevice in the slick trunk to stick a toe or a few fingers. Over and over, I tried and failed, followed by yet another slide down the trunk or the loss of my footing before making a quick leap beyond the snaky roots.

> The meaning that we attribute to things that happen can literally shape our stories and ultimately shape us.

This focused plotting might have normally been something to mention to the family at suppertime, but meals were quiet those days with everyone dealing with grief about the death of my grandmother in their own way. Maybe the goal of conquering this tree was my way. For fear I would be told not to try to climb it, I planned in silence. All I said at supper was "Amen" and "Pass the biscuits, please."

Day after day I twisted my body, jabbing my Chucks into a hole, until one day I finally grabbed a small knot and shimmied up one side and then another until I got a toehold and a grip high enough to barely reach that first huge branch jutting out of the tree's side. Now, if I could just hoist my body up onto that high, massive limb! With a deep breath and one more heroic effort, I had done it.

Straddling the big branch and enjoying the view from on high with pride, I contemplated the initials carved in the trunk and smiled. Yep, my best guess was that I was the youngest person and only girl! Even though I had forgotten to bring a pocketknife to add my own initials, it was a huge personal victory.

A Question from the Heart

HAVE YOU IDENTIFIED YOUR GOALS, AND DO YOU HAVE THE GUMPTION TO GO AFTER THEM?

One of the reasons we have imagination is to create dreams, to consider what you want and what you would like to do with your life. But dreams and goals can be tricky things. Dream too small, and you may never know your potential. Dream too big but without passion, and you may never work through the inevitable challenges that come with an aspirational goal.

Although Short Fuse would disagree, you may be thinking that my goals of climbing a tree or making the cheer squad were just silly little-kid goals—what about *real* life? But goals are relative. Goals, and the size of them, should change as you do.

Many people start with such huge goals that they give up before they get started. So, by sometimes thinking smaller in the beginning, you can get used to dreaming, trying, failing, trying again, and achieving, dreaming, trying, failing, trying again, and achieving. Then, when you identify a bigger goal that you are passionate about pursuing (which I hope you do!), just break it into smaller pieces and get back into the *process* until it becomes second nature—like a habit. That's right, the *habit* of *success*. Everyone who has ever achieved anything has had to learn this lesson.

Success in business is sometimes discussed in terms of climbing the corporate ladder, with each rung representing a new objective or level. I have never found a ladder to be the appropriate analogy for my career or my life, with its series of evenly divided steps heading in one direction. It leads you to believe that there are no surprises. Just one upward step at a time. Even in high heels, that's manageable. Right?

The truth is that résumés and life stories with strategically extracted sidesteps designed to create sequential bullet points carefully plotted in a consistent upward trajectory executed with precision like climbing a "ladder" rarely tell the whole story. While it is fine for people to summarize their CVs, it does not mean that there weren't ups and downs. You should not be dissuaded or incorrectly determine that you are headed in the wrong direction when you find yourself on a winding path with potholes. Most likely, every successful person's real-life path had potholes too.

Careers and life twist and turn. Everybody needs to plot their course and find the best way to *their* top. One day the path looks certain, and the next day that path no longer exists.

Why? Because there is no ladder. *Life is a beech.* A crazy-big, exciting tree with slick bark and lots of different ways to be scaled. You will try to climb it, and a limb might break off. You figure out another way up and get stuck. At weak moments, you look up and gain confidence by seeing some initials carved in the bark above the highest limbs. The key is to not remain among the snaky roots because you must stay dedicated to your goal and have the gumption to keep trying until you *climb your tree.*

Now, Create *Your* Story: Plant Your Goal Tree

First, you can't climb a tree unless you know what tree you are trying to climb. That is, you must know your objectives before you can embark on achieving them. It seems so obvious, but few people take the time to clarify their goals. Remarkably, that doesn't stop many from being confused and frustrated about what they have (or have not) accomplished in life. What if companies did that? No strategy, no financial objectives, no measurements or metrics. Well, they would nearly all fail. Why should it be different for people? Simply stated, know what you want.

Second, write down your goals and visualize them as if they are already a part of your life. I must have climbed that tree fifty times in my mind before I really did it. There is something inexplicable about the process of writing down your goals and visualizing them that increases the odds of you making the mental *decision* to achieve them and follow through.

Before you skip the writing part, consider the meaningful amount of research supporting this suggestion. *Forbes* has noted that this single action can increase your chances of success by up to 150 percent.[1] Additionally, a well-known Harvard Business School survey from

---

1   Mark Murphy, "Neuroscience Explains Why You Need to Write Down Your Goals If You Actually Want to Achieve Them," *Forbes*, April 15, 2018, https://www.forbes.com/sites/markmurphy/2018/04/15/neuroscience-explains-why-you-need-to-write-down-your-goals-if-you-actually-want-to-achieve-them/?sh=391bf9477905.

some years ago found that the 3 percent of a specific MBA graduating class who had written down their goals ended up earning ten times as much as the other 97 percent of the class in just ten years after graduation *put together*.[2] Seriously, why wouldn't you write them down?

After identifying your goals, writing them down, and visualizing the accomplishment of them, you must then have the gumption to stick with them. The word "gumption" is a little different from determination. Gumption is a mix of drive, passion, and creativity—not just sheer will. This is where the concept of being dedicated to your goals becomes important.

Finally, upon deciding which tree you want to climb, you don't have to have it *all* figured out. Your job is to grab the first limb—knowing that the twists, turns, and broken limbs are a natural part of the process. Fall down? Just get up and grab another limb.

With that, let's create your **Goal Tree** with a horizon of the next five years, and "plant it" in your mind (through the process of visualization).

> After identifying your goals, writing them down, and visualizing the accomplishment of them, you must then have the gumption to stick with them.

The tree trunk is made up of goals about *you*. You must take care of yourself *first*. Without a strong base, the entire tree will collapse. The stronger the trunk, the more branches that can be supported and the higher they can reach into the sky. These personal goals should cover

---

2   Sid Savara, "Why 3% of Harvard MBAs Make Ten Times as Much as the Other 97% Combined," sidsavara.com, accessed September 2021, https://sidsavara.com/why-3-of-harvard-mbas-make-ten-times-as-much-as-the-other-97-combined/.

areas and objectives designed to expand or improve your mind, your body, and your spirit. Perhaps start with two to three goals in each area.

After your personal goals are written, you can choose how many branches you want to create and how many stems are coming off the branches that represent subgoals, which is the process of breaking a big goal into smaller pieces so that it is more achievable. Most Goal Trees include branches like family, career, community, and finances.

Again, creating your Goal Tree is just the beginning. Then, plant it in your mind by visualizing the accomplishment of these goals and experiencing the feelings you will have when you do. Next? Grab that first limb!

GOAL TREE

IN FIVE YEARS I WILL ...

FAMILY   CAREER

FINANCES   COMMUNITY

MIND

BODY

SPIRIT

YOU

But Wait, There's More

While basking in my unlikely accomplishment astride that high limb after weeks of trying, I slowly realized that I was stuck. I did not know how to get safely back on the ground.

This was scary and dangerous. Descending the tall, slick trunk the way I came up was impossible. Jumping straight down into those snaky roots from this high perch would surely cause me to turn an ankle. I was in the midst of the Pine Woods and no one knew where I had gone, so the likelihood of someone hearing or helping me was low. And the sun was starting to set. I would get in trouble if I came home late. Plus, using the excuse that it was because I was stuck in a huge tree that I had no business climbing would not help the situation. As darkness threatened, I thought about my grandmother's passing, I thought about how worried my mom and dad would be about me, and I desperately looked for options as my heart raced and the screeching song of the cicadas mocked my dilemma.

After weeks of planning to get up the tree, I just had a half hour or so to figure out how to get down. Honestly, nothing looked that promising. Finally, I decided I had to try *something* as dusk slowly started to consume the Pine Woods. So I shimmied about fifteen feet on that massive branch out to where it was smaller and more flexible. I was hoping I could swing down and dangle with my arms while moving even farther toward the end of the limb. The plan was to use my weight to bounce on the limb and drop safely to the ground at the lowest point, far from the snaky roots. Deciding to drop down and hang by my arms was a worrisome decision, because I knew there would be no going back at that point—I would have to eventually let go, like it or not!

Although not perfectly executed, I swung down, bounced, and dropped to the ground, hitting hard enough to have to roll into the dry pine needles. After a quick brush-off, I ran out of the woods at top speed, arriving home just in time to slide through the screen door unnoticed.

Occasionally, as I am drifting off to sleep, my mind goes back to that time of change and challenge the summer my grandmother died. I walk past the vine-covered fence, jump across the narrow part of the creek, and trek through the open field until the green grass gives way to brown pine needles crunching under my sneakers. Is it just another childhood memory, or is there something more compelling about this story?

On contemplation, as innocent as this story seems, it poses a much larger question that I think has significantly impacted my life. After my tree-climbing adventure, I could have chosen to assess that experience in two very different ways:

1. **I should avoid setting challenging goals** because you never know what can happen, and it might turn out to be *bad*, or

2. **I should continue to set challenging goals** because you never know what can happen, and it might turn out to be *awesome*.

It is ironic that both potential lessons are based on the exact same facts. The difference is the story I chose to weave around the facts. The first version is limiting and defeatist, and the second is liberating and empowering.

The critical juncture was deciding (consciously or unconsciously) that the unexpected twist of getting stuck in this tree—which frightened and temporarily paralyzed me—was one of the best parts of the whole experience.

Because of the decision to label it as "awesome," I climbed the tree many times that summer, often just to shimmy to the end of the branch and swing down. Now, *that's* a life lesson. Indeed, a tree full of wisdom.

So if you want your life to be more exciting than a forest full of easy-to-climb pine trees, the key is to not only enjoy setting the challenging goals but to truly enjoy the process of achieving those goals even when things happen that you did not expect or plan. Maybe even things that you think could be labeled as bad.

The beautiful thing is, since the stories we weave around our life experiences are choices, not only can we consciously select empowering meanings for current events; we can also choose to "rewrite" stories to weave around events that have already happened. This is not about pretending to change the past. Facts are facts. This is about recognizing that *your perception or interpretation* of what those facts mean or don't mean to you can be limiting or liberating your belief structure—which in turn impacts your future choices and, therefore, your life.

After I became the CEO of Build-A-Bear, it was time once again to pause and set some goals that I would like to accomplish in my new role. Given that Build-A-Bear Workshop is a publicly traded company, one of my many objectives was to ring the bell at the New York Stock Exchange (NYSE). A few years later in 2017, the leadership team was asked to do just that in celebration of the company's twentieth anniversary. After the event, I was invited to sign my name on the walls in a room behind the podium, where CEOs and other "bell ringers" before me have left their mark, not unlike the carvings of the beech tree climbers from long ago. It was an honor to be listed among these businesspeople, especially the women, who had provided proof that my eventual goal of becoming a CEO was possible.

On the walk back to my hotel, I paused to pay homage to the *Fearless Girl* statue, which was then placed in front of the famous *Charging Bull* on Wall Street. Her hands-on-her-hips determination caused moments from my childhood to flash through my mind—

including photos of me in the same stance and my tree-climbing adventure the summer my grandmother died when I discovered (decided?) that setting goals that were "out of reach" was a good idea.

As I posed for a photo near the *Fearless Girl*, replicating her stance in front of the bull, I couldn't help but wonder if *her* father had nicknamed her Short Fuse too. But somehow, I'm sure that she will climb her impossible tree.

CHAPTER 2

Everywhere You Go, There You Are

Perspective & Possibility

The most important decision we make is whether we
believe we live in a friendly or hostile universe.
—ALBERT EINSTEIN

My Story

Folks in a small town can triangulate you based on "your people."
After a few questions, they can often identify your parents, your
grandparents, and what part of the county they were from, or if they
were from an adjacent county, or if they were just "not from around
here." Occasionally in the course of the conversation, details will be
filled in, like "Now, you might not know this, but I taught school
with your grandmother before you were born." After that, everything
is friendly, and the world is right.

Like most of us, I did what was expected, including going to church, being respectful, and likely because of my grandmother's influence, making sure I got good grades. However, when straight A's were reported, my dad would ask if I was having enough fun at school.

The big wooden desks in my grade school were carved with previous students' names and initials. And, just like the beech tree, you could identify some of them from years past. I believe these generational connections helped us feel like we belonged not just "in" our town but "to" our town, almost tied to it through the people and stories echoing from the past. But at an early age, I started to yearn for more. This dichotomy of feeling like I belonged there but wanting to explore created an odd sensation that is a little hard to explain. Contrary to the belief of some city folk, many people stay in, or come back to, the small community of their birth because they choose to, not because they couldn't *get out.*

Even my parents had moved away for a while to larger cities. But shortly before I was born, my father asked to have his job transferred with the telephone company so they could raise their children closer to family. As a part of this move, my mother decided to leave her job to be a stay-at-home mom until I was out of elementary school, eventually returning to work as the secretary for our church. They raised us with love and gave us more than we needed to have a fulfilling childhood.

So my wanderlust was somewhat of an anomaly and, therefore, a source of confusion for me and my family. Occasionally, my parents could not understand what was driving me—especially if it was destined to drive me farther from home. Even so, as I grew older, the desire to learn about and experience more of the world beyond the county line started to make the environment feel limiting, even frustrating.

Honestly, it took me many years to understand and really appreciate the value of being grounded, of having listened to and being able to pass down the family lore, of knowing where many generations of my ancestors are buried, simply of being *from somewhere.*

By the time high school rolled around, my extracurricular school interests had evolved beyond cheering and gymnastics. I participated in art, dance, drama, and numerous clubs. I was recognized for or elected to all sorts of things, and a large bulletin board hung in my purple bedroom overflowing with awards, newspaper clippings, dried corsages, and winning ribbons, medals, and certificates.

All of this, combined with my family roots, helped me feel a little like I was kind of *somebody* in my small town. Now, don't get me wrong—I believe it is important that everyone can grow up believing that they matter. That sense of purpose can be instilled by your town, your family, or a teacher, or it can be developed by participation in an activity or a sport—any of which can make a world of difference for building self-esteem in kids.

However, believing that I was *somebody* also had a downside when it came time to leave my community—especially since I knew that the place where I felt like a somebody, although wonderful, might mean I wouldn't be much of *anybody* somewhere else. No wonder I had a simultaneous sense of dread and excitement as senior year began and people started planning for the next stage in life.

I don't recall a lot of the kids in my high school visiting colleges their senior year, as many were simply planning on starting a job or getting married or just getting on with life. Conversely, I had always believed I would go to college, but there was not a clear plan. My parents hadn't attended university, so there was no advice or legacy. My ACT score was strong enough that it ultimately allowed me to skip many of my core freshman college courses, but I don't recall being counseled about my options. I do remember that my ASVAB (Armed Services Vocational Aptitude Battery) score prompted a visit from the military to recruit me, but that wasn't my path. Having a "short fuse" and a bit of a habit of making up my own rules would probably not bode well at boot camp! The only real filter was Dad telling me I had to pick a school with in-state tuition.

With that, early in my last year of high school, my thought for the following fall was to attend a smaller college that was fairly close to home in the middle of the state.

I don't remember being particularly excited about going. Maybe deep down I believed attending a smaller college would help me navigate or even avoid the rocky road that often comes along with the transtion that a person from a small town makes when they go to college, innately knowing that without successfully navigating across the chasm, I might become the subject of a verse in Bruce Springsteen's yet-to-be-released anthem "Glory Days."

Senior year was flying by, the football season had already ended, and we were looking forward to Christmas break. Then, as a part of my high school German language class, I was offered an opportunity to travel to Germany, Switzerland, and Austria a few months before graduation. But I had never been on a trip like that. I had never even been on an airplane!

I can understand why my dad wasn't thrilled with the idea of me flying across the ocean to Europe. But my mom was all for it. She was almost always the voice of encouragement when it came to opening my mind and thinking beyond where or how I had been raised.

Since he was conflicted about the idea and in disagreement with my mother, my dad sought the advice of my great-aunt and great-uncle, the sister and brother-in-law of his mom (my beloved grandmother who had passed away a few years before).

After a long conversation weighing the pros and cons of this potential international trip, my great-uncle finally said to my father, "I'm sure your mom would have wanted her to go."

That was the tipping point. Once again, on top of the funds that she had set aside for me to attend college due to the value she placed on education as a schoolteacher, the influence of my grandmother was impacting my life from beyond the grave. With her posthumous blessing, I boarded a plane for the first time in my life and headed for Frankfurt, Germany.

So much about that trip was life changing. Of course, I knew the rest of the world was out there. No kidding—it had only been a few summers before that I'd decided to read nearly an entire set of the Bicentennial Edition of our World Book Encyclopedias just to learn about it! Seriously, physically being on another continent, walking on the streets, and interacting with the people was a bit mind blowing for a wide-eyed teenager who had never left the southeastern United States.

It was a place that had more snow than I had ever seen in my entire life—put together. It was a place with buildings that were older than our country and majestic mountains that dwarfed the rolling hills of middle Tennessee.

But here's what really got me. As different as it was, and even though no one knew me and I knew no one, I was still *fine*. Imagine that. I was worried I might feel lost and alone so far away from my roots, but people were friendly and welcoming, even with my mediocre grasp of the German language.

It was the first time in my life I realized that all this mythology about who I was or wasn't didn't matter. I wasn't *somebody* anymore—but I also was not *nobody*. This experience did not lead to an existential crisis.

Yes, the world is much bigger than my hometown, but it didn't matter. The trip didn't make me feel small and insignificant. Conversely, it made me feel empowered and full of possibilities. If I could *get along* this far from home with people with a different background, country, culture, and language, I could go anywhere. All of a sudden, going to college, big or small, close to home or far away, wasn't so concerning anymore.

My dad used to tell me, "Wherever you go, there you are." But I had to travel forty-five hundred miles across an ocean to recognize that what he was saying is just a down-home version of some ancient Chinese philosophy. Who you are does not change just because you change your surroundings. You are the one person who you can never get away from. Sometimes that realization can be a good thing—like in my case of discovering that *who I was* would be just fine outside my comfort zone. But sometimes that can be a tough reality. If the same problems keep popping up in your life no matter where you go, maybe the best place to look is in the mirror. It is impossible for that kind of issue to be fixed by some*one* else, or some*where* else. What a gift to learn at the age of eighteen.

Upon my return from Europe, my goals quickly evolved to seeking out the best opportunity, as fast as I could, that would provide the broadest perspective and greatest possibility for my college experience. For me, this meant shifting my college sights to the biggest school I could find (with in-state tuition!), which was the University of Tennessee. I also decided that

> If the same problems keep popping up in your life no matter where you go, maybe the best place to look is in the mirror.

starting school the next fall quarter was too long to wait! I wanted to start that summer—right after high school graduation—which wasn't very far away.

The year was 1982, and almost unbelievably, not only was the World's Fair happening in the United States, it was being held in Knoxville, Tennessee, home of the University of Tennessee Volunteers! The fairground was being built adjacent to the college campus, and my focus quickly became to get accepted to UT for the summer and pick up a few courses while also working at the World's Fair, where over twenty countries from around the globe would be exhibiting.

I was accepted to the school and moved into a dormitory on the side of campus near the fair. Then, with a little help from my new dormmate, I secured a sales position at a gift shop, which was run by a family who owned a retail store in New Delhi, India. Inside the exotic-looking location was a vast selection of inlaid teakwood plates, brass trays, and decorative enamelware. Best of all, because the World's Fair attracted visitors from across the globe, I was able to interact with people from all sorts of places—while trying to sell them some cloisonné jewelry, of course. The owner and his family were very kind, and they generously exposed me to Indian culture and food, which I love to this day.

Best of all, as a World's Fair employee, I had a free pass to all the exhibits. One of my most memorable experiences was going to the popular China pavilion early one morning before visitors were allowed in the park. China's presence at the 1982 World's Fair was a big deal since the country had not participated in the event since the St. Louis World's Fair in 1904. As I stood in solitary silence gazing at rows of life-size terra-cotta warriors and horses that had recently been discovered buried in the tomb of the first emperor of China from the year 210 BCE, my life felt small, like an insignificant speck in time. But it simultaneously felt simply magnificent. It was a little like when you look up at an endless diamond-filled sky on a moonless night far from the city lights and think about how tiny we all really are. You can't help but ask, "Why am I here? What am I supposed to do with this life?"

Okay, maybe I didn't need to be trying to decipher my purpose as it relates to my place in the space-time continuum at this juncture. Although, just saying, in the span of one year, I had gone from being a small-town girl who had never been west of the Mississippi River or north of the Mason-Dixon Line to being exposed to things that had broadened my perspective, which, in turn, changed what I thought my possibilities in life could be.

My universe had opened up. And I liked it!

I can imagine myself thinking, *So, Professor Einstein, my answer to your proverbial question about the most important decision we can make in life is "Yes, I believe I live in a friendly universe."*

 # A Question from the Heart

IS YOUR PERSPECTIVE LIMITING YOUR POSSIBILITIES?

There is often an interesting correlation between the way you respond to Einstein's famous quote about the universe and what you think about your own *you*niverse. That is, what we believe about ourselves is often simply the same opinions that we are reflecting onto the world around us. That's the real "why" behind the saying, "Wherever you go, there you are."

With that understanding, it becomes even more important that you think about any of the limiting or negative beliefs that you may have about yourself, because it takes more than external exploration to broaden your perspective and see your possibilities—it takes internal exploration, as well.

When you consider the kinds of beliefs you may have, it is important to acknowledge that you are likely harboring not only those you have *created* in your own mind but those that someone else may have said to you. If you are purposefully or accidentally carrying around some of these limiting beliefs or labels as a part of your personal story, odds are they are filtering what you see as your possibilities. In short, look in that mirror again and see if you are dragging around some imaginary negative mental baggage that could literally be weighing you down as much as choosing to ridiculously overpack for a multicountry European tour that ultimately limits the places you can visit and the things you can do.

Unfortunately, it is not always easy to put down our personal limiting luggage and walk away. We have created a life around this bag of beliefs. So we keep lugging it around—even though it is not doing us one bit of good.

Lots of big stuff can be in this bag, most of it being larger self-destructive constructs we have created over time (some linking all the way back to childhood) about what we can or cannot do in life because of who we are or are not and what we have or don't have. This bag can also include small habitual statements many of us use daily. Be aware. Tiny negative self-talk can be as destructive as those larger destructive beliefs. For example, in a moment of personal frustration, is your self-talk "*I am* so stupid" or "*That was* so stupid"? Trust me, no one should be defined by a brief moment of less-than-brilliant decision-making about a minor issue. Be careful what you say after "I *am*"—your subconscious is listening, and your bag has lots of side pockets.

On the contrary, Healthline noted that positive self-talk can enhance your general well-being, highlighting that people who engage in negative self-talk generally tend to be pessimists while the positive self-talkers tend to be optimists.[3]

Being labeled an optimist has received a bit of a bad rap, with the claim that those who think this way must be naive. However, a general belief that the universe is friendly and that your *you*niverse is amazing can have a real impact on your success and general well-being in life by increasing your resilience and passion, according to *Fast Company*.[4] Plus, wouldn't you improve the odds that you were having "enough fun" or at least just be happier in life if you didn't have to drag all that limiting belief, negative self-talk, and pessimism around in a big heavy bag? Don't believe me? Maybe you're a pessimist.

To successfully leave the bag behind, it's important to understand the real reason many of us drag it around in the first place. Like any bag that we overpack, there may be some stuff in there that's handy, but we all know it's not really *needed*. How can limiting beliefs be *handy*, you may ask? Well, if those unflattering labels or narrow ideas you have concocted about your potential *were true*, you get to continue to use them as excuses to not consider or go for any of the wonderful possibilities in life beyond your current bag of limiting beliefs, don't you? Let's face it: it will require some personal responsibility and bold change if you decide to own the fact that your *true* potential may be a whole lot bigger than what's in your bag.

I am a frequent flyer now, but I remember my first transcontinental flight to Germany very well. I listened intently to the flight atten-

---

3   Kimberly Holland, "Positive Self-Talk: How Talking to Yourself Is a Good Thing," Healthline, updated June 26, 2020, https://www.healthline.com/health/positive-self-talk.

4   Aaron Pitman, "Survival of the Happiest: How Optimism Affects Your Chances of Success," *Fast Company*, January 14, 2014, https://www.fastcompany.com/3024794/survival-of-the-happiest-how-optimism-affects-your-chances.

dant's instructions. It was made clear that we should leave our bags behind in case of emergency. Basically, in a life-or-death situation, you do *not* want to be burdened with that extra stuff. This is that same thing. You must be willing to leave that baggage behind. And, yes, we *are* talking about your life.

If you are not sure what's in your bag, unzip it and look underneath the neatly folded "can't/because" items. That is, whenever you say "I *can't* do this *because* …" or "I *can't* be this *because* …" the completion of these sentences is likely representative of some of your limiting beliefs.

Once you identify these beliefs, you may want to revisit your Goal Tree to make sure you were not modifying objectives because of your preconceived limitations. Why? Because not only does that extra baggage impact your ability to reach your current goals; it can also impact the quality of the goals you have set in the first place!

It is common knowledge that you must pay extra to carry additional baggage on a flight. Well, are you willing to pay the price of never reaching your goals because you would not leave the big bag of limitations behind?

While you are at it, please leave behind the Duffel of Doubt, Suitcase of Cynicism, Backpack of Blame, and Handbag of Hate too. They will only drag you down.

Now, Create *Your* Story: Make One Hundred Wishes

With a changed perspective, no negative baggage, and a friendly universe of possibilities, it seems like a perfect time to write a stream of consciousness list of **One Hundred Wishes for Life**, doesn't it?

Write a list of accomplishments that you would love to have made before your physical body says farewell to this friendly universe. (Some people call it a bucket list.) This list can consist of places you would like to visit, people you would like to meet, things you would like to achieve, awards you would like to win, and experiences you would like to have. This exercise is meant to be different from identification of your five-year goals using the Goal Tree in Chapter 1. The One Hundred Wishes is for *life* and often includes exciting one-off things like learning another language (maybe German?), visiting every state, touring a foreign city (like Frankfurt?), meeting a famous person, running a marathon, or climbing a mountain.

You may have an inclination to write something like "make a lot of money," but money is just a means to an end. What's the end? Why do you want to make a lot of money? Is it because you want to go somewhere? Where? Is it because you want freedom? Freedom to do what? If you still want to put down something about money, make sure it's specific, like a certain amount per year or a net worth goal.

If you are struggling to write anything, ask yourself what is keeping you from making big wishes. Did you really put that bag of limiting thoughts away? Come at this with a free spirit! Kids generally don't have much of a problem writing a list of wishes, do they? Well, it's mostly because they haven't had time to pack their bags yet.

If you are thinking this is a waste of time, you might be interested that the venerated college football coach Lou Holtz did a similar exercise when he was twenty-eight years old. He wrote down 107 things he wanted to accomplish in life. At the time, he was without a job and financially struggling with a third child on the way. He crammed his list with bold ideas like winning a national championship in college football, meeting the pope, and having dinner at the White House. To date, now well into his eighties, he has reportedly accomplished 103 of the items on the original list.

So have a little fun, use your imagination, and start writing your list without thinking too much. You might learn something about yourself! Give yourself thirty minutes to complete your list. That is only eighteen seconds per wish, so don't dally. Let it flow! Whatever you write, just remember—wherever you go, there you are. But you do not have to drag a great big useless bag of limiting beliefs along with you.

100 WISHES FOR LIFE

WRITE ONE HUNDRED AMAZING THINGS YOU WILL
DO, PLACES YOU WILL VISIT, PEOPLE YOU WILL
MEET, AND ACCOMPLISHMENTS YOU WILL MAKE
BEFORE YOU LEAVE THIS FRIENDLY UNIVERSE.
YOU HAVE THIRTY MINUTES TO *WISH*.

1. _____

2. _____

3. _____

4. _____

5. _____

6. _____

7. _____

8. _____

9. _____

10. _____

11. _____

12. _____

13. _____

14. _____

15. _____

16. _____

17. _____

18. _____
19. _____
20. _____
21. _____
22. _____
23. _____
24. _____
25. _____
26. _____
27. _____
28. _____
29. _____
30. _____
31. _____
32. _____
33. _____
34. _____
35. _____
36. _____
37. _____
38. _____
39. _____
40. _____

100 WISHES FOR LIFE

41. _____
42. _____
43. _____
44. _____
45. _____
46. _____
47. _____
48. _____
49. _____
50. _____
51. _____
52. _____
53. _____
54. _____
55. _____
56. _____
57. _____
58. _____
59. _____
60. _____
61. _____
62. _____
63. _____

64. _____

65. _____

66. _____

67. _____

68. _____

69. _____

70. _____

71. _____

72. _____

73. _____

74. _____

75. _____

76. _____

77. _____

78. _____

79. _____

80. _____

81. _____

82. _____

83. _____

84. _____

85. _____

86. _____

100 WISHES FOR LIFE

87. _____

88. _____

89. _____

90. _____

91. _____

92. _____

93. _____

94. _____

95. _____

96. _____

97. _____

98. _____

99. _____

100. _____

But Wait, There's More

My experiences in Europe and at the World's Fair exposed me to other countries, cultures, and ideas beyond my small hometown. Emotionally, intellectually, and even spiritually, I was changing my perceptions about myself and my environment.

Although my background is an inseparable part of my identity, it is not *who* I am, nor does it predetermine *what* I can do or be. So I left the limiting attributes I had associated with that in a bag and walked away. They would always be a part of my personal story, but they would not define my story.

As my mind and journey expanded, I can understand why my dad may not have wanted me to venture too far from home. It was not because he didn't love me. It was because he *did*. He was concerned for me, but he was assessing my life through his personal filters and, yes, even possibly his own limiting beliefs. This can be difficult to process, but it is not uncommon for the people closest to you to struggle with and not completely understand your dreams and ambitions, especially if they are vastly different from their own.

However, it is not that he wanted me to live a life without reaching for my goals. Both he and my mom often told me I could do anything I put my mind to. They encouraged me to try new things at a very young age. I just don't think they expected me to take their advice so seriously!

One summer evening when I was about six years old, we were enjoying some cool drinks on the swings that graced the wraparound porch of my grandmother's house. As darkness fell, the lightning bugs began to blink their glowing beacons, which naturally lured the kids into the large yard.

My brother was catching more lightning bugs than me, so I asked my dad for help. "You're too close to the porch lights," he said. "You've got to go out farther, beyond the oak trees." But he could tell I was concerned about venturing out where the light faded into the pitch country black.

"Now listen, Sharon," he said as he took my Ball jar to poke a few more air holes in the lid with his pocketknife, "you'll never catch the light until you're willing to step into the dark."

Simple words of wisdom.

I cautiously walked to the edge of the yard and peered beyond the big oaks where the porch lights dissolved into darkness. I could feel my heart pounding as I stepped beyond the trees. Almost magically, I was then easily able to fill my jar with lightning bugs!

Changing your perspective can be hard, but it is a necessary part of unlocking your true possibilities. Often it requires you to step into the dark, or the unknown, which is difficult to do if you are harboring limiting ideas about yourself or believe the universe is *hostile*.

> Changing your perspective can be hard, but it is a necessary part of unlocking your true possibilities.

The lightning bugs had been there all along, you know; I just couldn't see them until I was brave enough to change my perspective—and then catching the light became possible.

CHAPTER 3

The Back Road Not Taken

Clarity & Conviction

> *Clarity of mind means clarity of passion, too.*
> —BLAISE PASCAL

My Story

"Look to your left. Look to your right. Only one of you will graduate."

That's an ominous prediction to make in front of thousands of incoming students, but that's exactly what a school official said during my fall orientation at the University of Tennessee.

I had just returned to Knoxville, following a short break after my mind-opening summer working at the World's Fair, to now be told that the odds of me walking across the stage to receive a college diploma in four years were not in my favor.

As I sat in a sea of incoming freshmen who represented just a portion of the roughly thirty thousand students enrolled that fall, I couldn't help but recall some of my concerns about going to a large university in the first place. I also had a flashback of my first University of Tennessee Volunteers football game over a year before. Neyland Stadium is the fifth largest in the country, and even back then it could house nearly one hundred thousand people, which, for comparison, is larger than any NFL football stadium. I'm not sure why, but somewhere between the band's intermittent outbursts of our fight song, "Rocky Top," I decided to count the number of seats in the rows and columns of a particular section to see where my entire town of seven thousand people could sit if they all came to the game. Almost everyone I had ever known up until that point in my life could fit comfortably in one small section. But here I was at this big school, listening to this grim forecast about my imminently doomed college career.

After the initial wave of panic, I shook it off. I had to! I was going to be just fine! I subtly glanced at the two people sitting to my left and right in the packed auditorium and mustered up the bold thought, *Well, if that's the way it's gotta be, I'm gonna be the one that graduates!*

That's right, I had already been at UT for a quarter. I knew the ropes. I had some school credits under my belt and some work experiences that had contributed to a new perspective and expanded possibilities! Of course I would graduate! Plus, a few of my high school friends from back home were joining me for the fall quarter. Four of us had decided to be suitemates in one of the freshmen dormitories. Having them around was going to be fun and morally supportive.

It all started out great. We decorated our dorms and went to classes. We attended football games and frat parties. But well before it was time for anyone to walk across a stage, all three of my freshman suitemates had decided to leave UT.

Everybody has a different path to take, and what's right for one person isn't necessarily right for another. Some people might be better suited for a smaller college or decide that it is time to get married, or join the military, or get a job that doesn't require a college education. Until you walk in another person's shoes, you can't begin to know what is and isn't the right decision for them. All my original suitemates have beautiful lives, so ultimately leaving UT may have been the right decision for them. But at the time, it just felt disappointing and confusing for me.

As I watched each of them pack their dormitory belongings and drive away, the confidence I had mustered at orientation was no longer there, and, quite suddenly, nothing felt certain anymore. I didn't want to leave college, but I couldn't help but wonder why staying at the University of Tennessee would be right for *me*, if it was not right for my friends.

Despite having done so well in my classes, even my beloved art and architecture major that had been my dream for years was called to question. It was beyond me that I could now be confused about my friends, my major, my college, and my long-term goals. Maybe I was not who I thought I was after all. I was sick to my stomach as the famous line in a Clash song kept running through my head: "Should I stay, or should I go?"

Then, I made a decision that was shocking even to me. I opted to take a quarter off and move back home. I told myself that I just needed to hit the reset button. I needed to be back on familiar ground, at least for a little while, and then I would go back to college.

As much as I did not want to admit it, I had seen this movie before—and so had everyone else in my town. And deep down I knew that my chances of returning to UT after leaving were even worse than my terrible odds of graduating, based on the data shared on the first day of orientation.

While at home, I hung out with some old high school buddies and picked up a credit or two at a local community college. To make a little money, I eventually got a job working the night shift at the local blue jean pick-and-pack facility, boxing up jeans to ship to places like Walmart or JCPenney.

This could have easily been the end of my aspirational college story, as it is for many. You make a promise to yourself that some detour is "only for a little while." You get used to the routine. Days turn into weeks, which turn into months, which turn into years, and before you know it, your big plans are history, and your temporary diversions have become your life.

"And then Sharon packed her dreams into a cardboard box, drove it home from college, and tucked it away in a dark corner of her parents' attic in the three-bedroom ranch house where she had lived all her life. Her legacy: she looked to the left, she looked to the right, and the dropout was her. The end."

Blue jean pick-and-pack paychecks came and went. And then, some coworkers decided to give me a little advice. They let me know that I needed to slow it down. I was throwing off the productivity curve by picking and packing too efficiently. I was making them look bad. I'll admit that in my fresh-faced naivety, I was aghast. Not in front of them, but in my head. It took a while to process this information. When it finally sank in, it was a wake-up call. Some old short-fuse determination kicked in—the same determination of that little girl with her hands on her hips or that kid who'd climbed the impossible tree. I had made a promise to *myself*. There was *no way* I was giving up my dream (or my grandmother's dream for me) without, well, an ole college try.

I reconnected with the passion I'd felt when I had returned from Europe. I tried to get in touch with the confidence I'd had during that orientation speech. Heck, I remembered that my high school senior class song was "Don't Stop Believing," by Journey!

And then I realized that maybe part of *my* journey was to go back home before I could go on with life. Maybe this sidestep had accidentally provided the clarity required to never doubt my dreams again, maybe like "don't stop believing; hold on to that feeling," even if things get confusing.

Yes, unfortunately, sometimes we need to experience what we *don't* want before we can get a clear grasp of what we *do* want. Contrast creates clarity. Emotion can create motion. Don't you have an obligation to yourself to transform that sick pit in your stomach about something you don't want into a burning passion in your heart about something you do want?

That aching in your belly might be trying to tell you something about your life (assuming you didn't eat too much bad delivery pizza in your college dorm). Yes, your gut may know more than your brain does about what your heart really desires. Some researchers have called the ecosystem in our stomachs the "second brain." It's composed of one hundred million neurons, and, according to Johns Hopkins University, it sends information to your brain through something called the enteric nervous system.[5] Your brain can overthink things, but your gut often innately knows when you're on the wrong path. That's why we call it a "gut feeling."

> Sometimes we need to experience what we *don't* want before we can get a clear grasp of what we *do* want.

The more the "advice" of these coworkers echoed in my head, the more my gut was sending me a message. Why *wouldn't* I try? Why *wouldn't* I push myself? Why *wouldn't* I want to do the best job I could do? I enjoyed figuring out how to beat my previous day's numbers.

Do I think they were trying to teach me a lesson? Yes, but it wasn't the lesson I learned. To be clear, this is not commentary about being a pick-and-pack worker. That is a high-demand job, which is challenging and critical to our economy. In fact, I learned a lot of invaluable lessons by being on a pick-and-pack floor that have been beneficial in

---

5 "Your Second Brain," *John Hopkins Health* no. 28 (April 2, 2015), https://www.hopkinsmedicine.org/news/publications/johns_hopkins_health/spring_2015/your_second_brain.

my career from working with manufacturing plants around the world to being responsible for fulfillment and distribution centers. But the most important insight came from realizing what I wanted out of life. I wanted a job and coworkers that supported my dreams and pushed me to be the best I could be. And I wanted to be around people who also wanted to be the best that they could be. In this case, these particular people, regardless of the job, were trying to teach me that mediocrity should be my goal.

Was I really "just a small-town girl living in a lonely world" who, in the face of some coworker pressure, would lower her (pick-and-pack productivity) bar and decide not to go back to college? No. That was it. Deep down I knew I was not a quitter. I'd just needed to be reminded. I stood up and put my hands on my hips. I cashed my last paycheck, selected a new college major, and headed back to Knoxville.

 # A Question from the Heart

DO YOU HAVE ENOUGH CLARITY ABOUT YOURSELF TO LIVE WITH CONVICTION?

You know the old adage, "If you don't stand for anything, you will fall for everything"? These days a wide variety of research studies support the idea that *standing for something* or knowing your values can enhance your life and help you through tough situations. Identifying and living your values can lead to stress reduction, improved decision-making (including wiser career choices), better health habits, and increased confidence, according to *Psychology Today*.[6]

Without values, what will you use to filter all the decisions you will be required to make in your life? How can you expect to achieve

---

6   Meg Selig, "9 Surprising Superpowers of Knowing Your Core Values," *Psychology Today*, November 27, 2018, https://www.psychologytoday.com/us/blog/changepower/201811/9-surprising-superpowers-knowing-your-core-values.

your goals and dreams while also becoming the person you aspire to be without knowing your core values?

Dad once told me at a point of confusion that life's decisions are often not as "gray" as people like to pretend. People can make things complicated even when they already know the right choice deep down—they just don't want to make it, because it's hard or unpopular.

Given my childhood history of being determined, perhaps if I had already overtly embraced my value of perseverance, I may have stayed in college at that volatile and confusing moment after my suitemates decided to leave. If I had identified that value as a personal filter, my self-talk would have likely been something like "I'm no quitter. That's not who I am. I persevere—I will find a way. Of course I'm not dropping out!" However, I was conflicted because I could not easily recognize who I really was in the middle of my personal confusion.

Understanding and embracing what you stand for really does matter. Not having any established values can make decisions a lot more difficult than they should be, especially when you are under pressure. And that is when you need to know your values the most.

Now, Create *Your* Story: Define Your Values

It is time to create some clarity about what kind of person you think you are and want to become. I'm not talking about who you are based on a career, a title, a net worth, a nationality, a religion, a spouse, a parent, or some letters in front of or behind your name. I'm talking about when all of that is stripped away, what are your personal *values*? Who are *you*? Who are you striving to be *inside*?

This activity is fundamentally different from writing your goals and dreams. This exercise will require some self-assessment and soul searching to complete. Look to your metaphorical left and right—only one of you will do the exercise below. Is it gonna be you?

Deciding on your big conceptual guardrails and identifying your personal values is an empowering process. Many people already have a sense of their values, but few take the time to clarify them, write them down, and consciously live by them—with conviction. You can think about your values as the roots of your Goal Tree. They stabilize you and enable your dreams to branch out and reach high in the sky.

By the time I returned to UT, I had a much better sense about who I was—or who I was going to allow myself to be—and who I was *not*. I was setting new standards for myself, but I could not have articulated exactly what that meant at the time.

After I secured my new advertising major, I took several marketing courses over the next few quarters. In one of those classes, I was introduced to a well-known concept called the price/value equation. In a nutshell, it's about determining what goods and services are truly *worth* to consumers. That is, what *price* are consumers willing to pay for something based on how much *value* they place on the products you're offering? That value isn't always utilitarian or functional—it's also often intangible. It can be based on status or how something makes a consumer feel. As an example, it's why people will pay exorbitant amounts to wear a certain clothing brand even though the basic utility of a shirt is the same as one you could buy at a mass merchandiser.

Because my last name was Price at the time, after the class I started thinking about my own personal PRICE/values. Again, not specific objectives that I wanted to achieve but who I wanted to be—my guiding principles, so to speak.

I examined some common themes that were persistent in my life that had been of benefit to me, like perseverance, which I had evolved from a less beneficial tendency of being stubborn. I thought about the things that my parents had taught me. I studied attributes common to success and correlated them to ideas that felt authentic to me. Then, I checked them all with the one hundred million neurons in my enteric nervous system (my gut check).

Each letter, P-R-I-C-E, was envisioned as standing for a quality or characteristic. My plan was to use these attributes as a filter for decision-making in the largest and smallest ways, believing that they would help create intangible value in my life beyond any skills or facts I would eventually master or acquire. With that, I wrote my first set of PRICE/values, which went something like this:

PERSEVERANCE.
I will persevere in the pursuit of my dreams and goals.

RESPECT.
I will respect myself and others.

INTELLIGENCE.
I will live my life intelligently and always be willing to learn.

CREATIVITY.
I will use my gift of creativity to enhance everything I do.

EXCELLENCE.
I will always strive to be the best that I can be.

My PRICE/values have morphed through the decades, as well they should. It's an exercise I still use to set higher or, sometimes, more evolved standards for myself.

Over the years, in the face of thousands of options, I have contemplated questions like "Am I *persevering*, or am I giving up too quickly? Is this company a place where I *respect* the leadership and what the company stands for? Is this an *intelligent* decision? Is there any way to approach this problem more *creatively*? Is this action moving me one step closer to *excellence*?" I have turned down job interviews, dates, and opportunities where I could quickly decide "no" because the company, the guy, or the decision was not aligned with my PRICE/values.

Note that your values should not just govern the *big* choices in life—they should inform the small ones. And while I have not always made the *right* choice, when I don't, I know it almost immediately because I am tuned in to my values and I listen to my gut. Truthfully, I don't recall fretting over the decisions I have made that were guided by my values. Neither do I recall regretting them.

From my experience, it is helpful to use your name as an acronym when identifying your values because it creates a natural mnemonic device; plus, it makes it *personal*. To get started, list some attributes that are aspirational and/or inspirational to you. You may have more words than letters—but you will work it out.

These words don't have to accurately define you *now*. You are a work in progress, not a finished product. Ask yourself what kind of *person* you want to become. What type of *values* do you want to define and guide your life? What words would you want others to use when describing what kind of person you are—now and later in life?

Once you have decided on your value words, do a gut check and review them often, perhaps through verbal affirmations like "I am (insert each of your values here)." This *good* self-talk seeps into your subconscious just like the *bad* self-talk referred to before. But good self-talk doesn't weigh you down (with more baggage); it lifts you up.

By clarifying who you are deep down and the type of person you aspire to become, you will more easily recognize what really matters to you—so future decisions can be made more quickly with greater clarity, less stress, more conviction, and little regret.

DEFINE YOUR VALUES

Choose an acronym, like your name, and write it vertically in the space below.

Visit www.storiesandheart.com for an alphabetical list of inspirational and aspirational words, or determine your own.

Choose words that represent your desired values and share the first letter of those in your acronym.

Fill in the areas beside the letters of your acronym with the words you chose.

From those, circle one word on each line; then put it into action and start consciously living your values.

Example:

N   Nice, Nurturing

A   Ambitious, Adventuresome

M   Motivated, Mindful

E   Excellence, Energetic, Empowered

DEFINE YOUR VALUES

Add your values to the roots of your Goal Tree in Chapter 1.

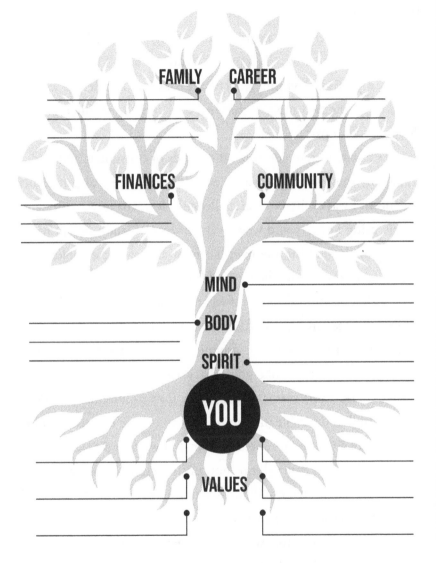

FAMILY   CAREER

FINANCES   COMMUNITY

MIND

BODY

SPIRIT

YOU

VALUES

But Wait, There's More

Reflecting upon my return to the University of Tennessee, I've often joked that I switched my major to advertising because, alphabetically, it was listed first among the options. Truth be told, I wanted to stay true to my original vision. Advertising was just a different kind of mash-up of the two subjects that had drawn me to architecture and design: art and psychology.

It's fascinating to get inside the minds of consumers and understand *why* they think the way they think (à la the real price/value equation). I was excited by the challenge of learning how to influence people using imagery and words. These areas of study also provided insights as to assessing my own behavior and thoughts objectively, which led to discovering how I could influence *myself*.

With a newfound clarity of what I *didn't* want and my PRICE/ values in place, another shift happened. I started to recognize the power created when you are driving *toward* something you deem positive and desirable (like going back to college because I was in pursuit of a dream) versus driving *away* from something you deem negative and undesirable (like going back to college because I wanted to get out of a job environment or a small town that seemed limiting to me). Whether I realized it or not, until then, many of my actions and choices had been more about avoiding a *negative* outcome because I did not want the alternative of the goal versus the pursuit of a *positive* outcome because I simply wanted to achieve the goal.

Of course, taking definitive and positive steps to get away from something undesirable is still action, and it is better than doing nothing. But real momentum in life starts when you clarify and begin taking steps, with conviction, toward something desirable. One is fueled by concern and fear, and the other is fueled by passion. Action

driven by the emotion of fear can be temporarily effective but ultimately draining. Action driven by the emotion of passion, on the
other hand, is endlessly invigorating.

Now that I was creating goals and using my PRICE/values filter
to clarify objectives that were more about what I *wanted* versus what
I *didn't want*, I started to contemplate "crazy" ideas that I would have
never considered before. For
example, I became bold enough to
consider a move to the mecca of
advertising, New York City, and
made sure to sign up for the annual
trip to Manhattan to visit agencies
with the UT Advertising Club. I
figured, where else would someone
whose personal values included
creativity and excellence want to
work if they were pursuing a career in advertising?

> **Real momentum in life starts when you clarify and begin taking steps, with conviction, toward something desirable.**

One of my favorite poems is "The Road Not Taken," by Robert
Frost. By now, you probably recognized the down-home take on the
poem with the title of this chapter, "The Back Road Not Taken."
The last lines of Frost's famous work are "Two roads diverged in a
wood, and I—I took the one less traveled by, and that has made all
the difference."

We all choose between lots of roads in life. In this story, the two
roads that diverged were choosing to go back to college or not. That
led to me changing my major to advertising, defining my personal
values, and shifting my objectives to be more about driving toward
something positive versus driving away from something negative. Was
it the road "less traveled by"? Well, at the very least, if you simply
consider that only about 30 percent of people in the United States

have a bachelor's degree, according to the US Census Bureau, you would have to say, statistically, yes.[7]

Since that time, many of my life choices have included the consideration of taking the road "less traveled by," and many times I have had the conviction and passion to take it.

A few years ago, I was compelled to visit Robert Frost's farm in New England. Walking around the property with my youngest daughter, I imagined that this was the actual "yellow wood" where the "two roads diverged" from the opening line as I recited the famous poem out loud, which ends with the following:

I shall be telling this with a sigh
Somewhere ages and ages hence:
Two roads diverged in a wood, and I—
I took the one less traveled by,
And that has made all the difference.

---

7   "U.S. Census Bureau Releases New Educational Attainment Data," US Census Bureau, March 30, 2020, https://www.census.gov/newsroom/press-releases/2020/educational-attainment.html.

CHAPTER 4

What's the Worst Thing That Could Happen?

Faith & Action

Throw your heart over the bar and your body will follow.
—NORMAN VINCENT PEALE

My Story

"I'll be back!"

With uninhibited gusto, I bellowed this famous line like a Southern-accented Schwarzenegger from the fifth-floor window of my room at the Roosevelt Hotel on East Forty-Fifth Street. In true New Yorker fashion, hardly anyone gave me a second glance, but I did not need their endorsement. I meant it!

It was my senior year in college and my first visit to Manhattan. The trip had been orchestrated by the University of Tennessee's Advertising Club to visit some of the city's top ad agencies, many of which were scattered up and down the industry's famed street, Madison Avenue.

The year was 1986, and remnants of the real-life *Mad Men* era still echoed through the halls of many of those agencies, as did the actual footsteps of the legends that created them. I was completely enamored.

After returning to Knoxville to walk across the stage to receive my college diploma (yes, it *was* me that graduated—with honors, to boot!), my eyes were fixed on the Big Apple.

But I wasn't the only one with dreams. Two friends in the UT Ad Club were also smitten by the city and its possibilities and had vowed to move there as well. They didn't make their declarations out of a hotel window, but they were just as serious. Almost immediately after graduating, they left me and our college town to take receptionist positions at two top ad agencies and moved into something called a "railroad apartment" in Hoboken, New Jersey.

As time went on, it was killing me that I had not fulfilled my promise to those confused New Yorkers on Forty-Fifth Street, even though the only person who still recalled my window declaration was me.

Of course, in my mind, I had lots of practical reasons for the delay of my return! First, even though it was a common way to break into the biz, I didn't want to start at an agency as a receptionist. Therefore, I thought I needed to get a little experience so I could start my New York ad career directly in the account management department. Second, I needed to save some money before my move.

So Knoxville remained my home, and I secured a position at a local advertising agency. My first job there was an assistant media buyer, literally with a desk in the copy room. I worked my way up to an account executive servicing local and regional businesses, which included doing everything from writing ad copy, to managing relationships, to planning marketing events—even playing an instrumental part in landing a rather large account for a new TV affiliate that was coming to the market. One of the best parts was that the owner of the agency had started his advertising career in New York years before, so I was a sponge when he discussed his early career experience there.

Deep down, however, I knew that you didn't tell New York City, "I'll be back," without every intention of going back, and NYC kept haunting me because of it. It was almost an annoying, even demanding, call. I couldn't shake it. I was sick of imagining what the amazing lives of my friends must be like as they fearlessly chased their dreams in the city that never sleeps. Surely, every morning they would don their big-shouldered business clothes and catch the ferry across the East River from Hoboken, while the morning sun glinted off the buildings of Manhattan—no doubt accompanied by Carly Simon's "Let the River Run" playing somewhere in the distance—just like Melanie Griffith in the late '80s movie *Working Girl*.

Finally, one day I hit a tipping point. I decided that the pain of never knowing if I could *make it there* had become greater than the fear of trying.

Late in 1988, without one job interview scheduled, I decided not to sign the year-end renewal on my apartment in Knoxville and bought a plane ticket to New York City for the following January. My plan was to land a job at a Manhattan-based advertising agency in one week because that was all I could afford to take off work. Was that unrealistic? Absolutely. Did I completely understand how unrealistic? Not a clue.

This was my five-step plan for securing a job in the advertising industry in just one week:

1. Get my hands on a "Red Book"—otherwise known

> I decided that the pain of never knowing if I could *make it there* had become greater than the fear of trying.

as the *Standard Directory of Advertisers*—which had contact info for all the top advertising agencies in New York, along with their key personnel and titles. It was about three inches thick and filled with every name you might possibly need to break into the industry.

2. Put together a list of the top agencies and identify some people to call from those agencies based on how *nice* their names sounded.

3. Cold call these people using my highly scientific "nice-person assessment" strategy. It is hard to imagine what some of them must have thought, picking up the phone to be greeted by a perky voice saying, "Hi, my name is Sharon Price, and I want to move to New York City and work in advertising. I was hoping you would help me." The plan included calling early in the morning so their receptionists or secretaries were less likely to be there to filter me out—thereby increasing the odds that the *nice* person would actually answer the phone directly.

4. After a short (yet charming!) chat, ask if I could mail my résumé directly to them. And not just that—ask if they would be willing to walk my résumé to the human resources department and hand deliver it once they received it. My logic was that if I blindly sent my résumé to the human resources (HR) department, it would probably end up in a dump bin. But if somebody in house walked it there, well, then I had a shot.

5. A week or so later, call the agency's HR department and inquire about my résumé, mentioning my new "friend" (the *nice* employee who had agreed to hand deliver it to them for me). I believed that having this connection increased my potential of getting an actual in-person meeting.

When speaking with HR, it was critical to share that I already had plans to be in New York and I would love to stop by the office, even if it was just for informational purposes. No need to fly me there since I already had my ticket. Plus, I wasn't asking for an interview, so getting a yes should be easy. I just wanted to sit down with somebody and talk about what was involved in the job and learn about the industry.

Bonus information: It is amazing how many people will find fifteen or twenty minutes if you're genuine and not asking for anything but to have a cup of coffee and learn about their industry, their company, and their career.

At the conclusion of the five-step plan, I had scheduled three meetings per business day during that weeklong trip to New York the last week of January. That's fifteen interviews in five days. I figured, Manhattan is a small island, only a few miles wide and thirteen or so miles long. I should be more than up to the task of making it to all my appointments on time. To level set, all of this was done in a time of hand-typed letters—no cell phones, texts, or email—written appointment calendars, and no GPS to help me find my way to an appointment once I was up there. No problem.

Next on the list was to find a place to stay. By this time, one of my friends from the Hoboken apartment had moved into a single room at a women-only residence in Manhattan. The best she had to offer me was a smidge of space to sleep on her floor—I took it. At night, we would discuss our plans to get an apartment together in New York after I got a job. Assuming, of course, I did.

This creative or crazy strategy, depending on your point of view, had not popped into my head naturally. Partially to build up some self-assurance to fulfill my Manhattan personal pledge, I had been reading a famous book called *The Power of Positive Thinking*, by Norman Vincent Peale. Although it is mostly a faith-based work and was already decades old by that time, some of the concepts in the book really spoke to me in ways beyond any specific dogma. I was especially intrigued by Peale's idea of "throwing your heart over the bar." I interpreted that as being brave enough to take definitive action only on faith or belief in a dream. That is, to do something *physical*—like buying a plane ticket or not renewing a lease—*before* there was any evidence (like a scheduled interview) to do it. By the time I boarded the plane to LaGuardia with my big, chunky, totally packed appointment book, the pages of this small pink paperback were dog eared and covered with notes scribbled in the margins to encourage me to stay positive through the process.

Zigzagging across the city day after day from appointment to appointment was harder than I anticipated. This little island was a lot bigger than I'd imagined! I was extra exhausted from sleeping on the floor, and the only thing that my pavement pounding was producing seemed like a whole lot of "we will get back to you" or "we aren't looking for anyone right now." I was losing hope as Friday approached. Maybe this positivity thing wasn't so powerful after all? By the end of the week, my feet were killing me, but finally, one of those fifteen meetings had led to a sixteenth. It was a follow-up interview with DDB/Needham Worldwide, the huge agency known for a wide array of well-known accounts, legendary advertising slogans, and iconic ad industry titans.

Almost everything about my second interview at DDB is still clear in my mind. I was wearing a red wool double-breasted suit and my last clean silk blouse, which I had accessorized with a bold gold-tone chain necklace. Since I had studied art and architecture in college, I remember that the chairs in the glimmering white lobby at 437 Madison Avenue looked a lot like leather Mies van der Rohe "Barcelona" chairs, which are ridiculously expensive. I kept repositioning myself, so I was sitting on the very edge of the black tufted cushion with my back straight, knees neatly together, and feet properly crossed at the ankles—just like my grandmother had taught me years earlier. I wondered if she would be proud of me.

I tried to look calm and natural as the heels of a few DDB associates clicked across the shiny marble floors while they chattered away about this or that advertising account, bringing me back to the weighty reality of the moment. I glanced down at my conservative low-heeled pumps and checked the time. I thought about how I had made payments for months to buy this tiny Gucci watch with a black leather band through a special credit card offering because I had read a story about a guy who wanted a job in New York, so he spent his last dollar on an expensive tie. That way, he said, it didn't look like he was desperate for the position. That made sense to me.

My dream was within my grasp. One company had called me back for another conversation. What were the odds of that happening? Probably pretty bad. But clearly not impossible. Because it *did* happen. And I was sitting in the lobby potentially awaiting the opportunity of a lifetime!

Breathe. Think positively! Just one more interview.

The receptionist escorted me to the HR offices for DDB. The recruiter explained the specifics of the account executive training program. She said it was a yearlong process with rotations through different departments at the agency, like media buying and creative. The program also included attending informational luncheons and seminars on important skills like public speaking with the other trainees already in this class.

Because it was late January and other trainees had already started in the fall of the previous year, the program was well underway. I'd be playing catch-up.

I told her I was ready and eager to accept the position. "That's great," she said. "We'll call later to solidify the offer."

I sat in silence. I had rehearsed and visualized this moment multiple times. I hadn't just thrown my heart over the bar—I had thrown it clear over the Brooklyn Bridge. I wasn't leaving Manhattan, I wasn't even leaving this *office*, without a firm offer.

"Why can't you just make me the offer now?" I blurted.

Her eyes widened. She was not expecting that.

"Listen," I continued, "I have already let my apartment go in Tennessee, and I'm moving to New York whether you give me a job or not. Someone will, but I'd rather work here. What else do you need to know to make me an offer right here, right now? Let's just get this done."

She looked back at me. Silence.

A Question from the Heart

ARE YOU WILLING TO TAKE ACTION BASED ONLY ON THE FAITH IN YOUR GOALS?

The two reasons people don't take action to achieve their goals are that they either don't really believe achieving their goal is possible (lacking faith) or they are afraid of the pain associated with the potential of failure (having fear).

First, the fear is real, and it is not "all in your head." It is also *physiological*. You can *feel* it in your body. The same types of chemicals that are released in the brain in response to actual situations where we should be on high alert are released when we *imagine* these potential terrible outcomes—as if the hypothesized outcomes are real threats.

The key to conquering what is often an overassessment of the danger is to acknowledge the fear and then shelve the paranoid scenarios. If you can't do this, you won't be "throwing your heart over the bar"—you'll be throwing your dreams out the window. Enter the impetus for the title of this chapter: "What's the worst thing that could happen?"

Just ask yourself, "What *is* the *worst* that could happen?" if you take this or that action in faith. *Really.* Most of the time it's just not that scary. Work through it logically.

For my trip to New York City, after I ignored things like "the plane could crash" or "they might laugh me out of the building," I finally assessed that the worst thing that could happen was more like "I don't get a job, and I don't move to New York." That was it.

I would have had to swallow my pride, but I would just go back to my ad job in Knoxville, and I am sure I could find another studio apartment. By no means is that a life-threatening or career-ending situation. At least I could stop torturing myself about not even trying to fulfill the promise I made to New York City—and myself. Plus, I would have had a trip to Manhattan to see an old school friend. That's a pretty decent outcome (despite having slept on the floor).

Another trick is to simply relabel the fear. Believe it or not, the physiological response produced by fear is very similar to the response to the emotion of excitement. That's right—in many ways, your body cannot tell the difference between fear and excitement until *you* decide (based on the circumstances) which emotion it *should* be. According to *Psychology Today*, what really matters is how your brain labels the feeling.[8]

This was exemplified for me in a public speaking course during my DDB training program. The instructor was explaining how the

---

8   Amelia Aldao, "Why Labeling Emotions Matters," *Psychology Today*, August 4, 2014, https://www.psychologytoday.com/us/blog/sweet-emotion/201408/why-labeling-emotions-matters.

"butterflies in your stomach" and your heart racing right before you go on stage is fear, but not to worry because he was going to give us some tips and techniques to manage those discouraging feelings.

Well, this was a genuine shock to me. I had always thought that those feelings right before I stepped on stage were signaling the excitement and anticipation of making the presentation. I decided that guy did not have permission to relabel my feelings as something disempowering. *If I think the feeling is excitement, that is what it will be!* Little did I know at the time how right I was.

When you can understand and manage the fundamentals (and tricks) of fear, you have a lot more room for building your faith. Faith is different than hope. Hope is passive. Faith, as noted in my dog-eared pink paperback about positivity, is about action. It is about taking a definitive step toward the achievement of your goal even when you have no real evidence that it is achievable.

When you really believe that the goal is going to happen—that is, when you have the "power of positive thinking" on your side—your actions follow naturally. After deciding to get a job in New York City, *obviously* I would need a plane ticket to go there. So I bought one. Separately, what in the world would I do with an apartment in Knoxville since I was moving to Manhattan? So I did not renew my lease. It is perfectly logical.

When recounting this story, I often cap it off with the comment that "sometimes we do better when we don't know better." When we are younger, we often don't understand the odds; therefore, they *don't get in our way*. It is sort of like beginner's luck. As we grow older and "smarter," we weigh the stark reality of achieving a difficult goal, so the odds *do get in our way*, undermining our faith.

Honestly, sometimes, the worst thing you can do is calculate your odds. If every wannabe entrepreneur did that, given the US Small

Business Administration reports that over half of new businesses fail in the first five years, no one would ever start a new company![9]

In like manner, thousands of young people dream of moving to New York, many of them vying for the same job opportunities. I hardly knew anyone in the city, and advertising is an industry that thrives on connections. If I had really understood this situation strictly by the numbers, I never would have even boarded that flight to LaGuardia— let alone bought a ticket without one scheduled interview!

> Sometimes we do better when we don't know better.

So what made the chances of securing my dream job any better than others? It is hard to ignore that I may have tipped my own odds by taking action on nothing more than the faith that I would get a job. "Throwing my heart over the bar" changed my mindset, which changed my choices, which changed my odds, which changed my outcome. The irony is that I took actions that improved my odds, partially *because* I lacked the knowledge of how bad those odds were.

Aristotle noted, "It is part of probability that many improbable things will happen," which really means that someone will beat the odds. I'm just asking—Why not you? Real faith is not about understanding the odds; it's about learning when to strategically ignore them.

Remember, if all you do is live your life based on averages, that is just the life you will live. An average one.

---

9   US Small Business Administration, "Small Business Facts," June 2012, https://www. sba.gov/sites/default/files/Business-Survival.pdf.

Now, Create *Your* Story: Get Some Traction

Clearly, I am not telling you to just go buy a plane ticket and all your dreams will come true. But I am asking that you identify and take some of the actions that you would do normally, if you really had complete faith that achieving your goal was a fait accompli.

Yes, assessing the odds of a goal and then actively choosing to ignore them may sound counterintuitive, if not a little crazy. We have a strong inclination to approach our lives and careers with open eyes and thoughtful planning executed in an orderly fashion. However, the achievement of big goals in life often requires you to flip the process on its head. That is, you need to have enough faith to take definitive action toward the goal far before there is any proof whatsoever of its potential achievement.

If the odds were good and the outcome was guaranteed, everyone would do it. And if everyone could do it, then the odds would not be long. Let's face it; just look across history—the most remarkable goals were not easily achieved. So maybe you just have to decide that the odds don't matter. That's right. The. Odds. Don't. Matter.

> **The achievement of big goals in life often requires you to flip the process on its head.**

Sports teams do this all the time. They know the betting odds—that is, the "collective knowledge" of their potential to win, down to the minute. There is not an underdog coach on the wrong side of the betting line who hasn't told the team, "The. Odds. Don't. Matter. Get out there and play your heart out. Play like you're gonna *win!*"

Often, they lose. But just ask anyone who has ever been on or rooted for a "Cinderella team"—sometimes they *do* win because it *is* possible! And *that's* what matters.

For this chapter's activity, please review your Goal Tree and your One Hundred Wishes list. Then, pick some things that will really require you to have some faith to make it happen. Things where you think the odds are against you. Objectives where you know you will have to "throw your heart over the bar" to ever have a chance. Put these goals and wishes on the chart on the next page.

Adjacent to these grand goals, add one tangible action you will make toward achieving each goal and identify the date by which you will do it. Prove to yourself that you have enough faith in your dream to take action toward the achievement of it! You might be surprised how much *traction* you can create by taking one *action* based in faith. Struggling? Well, what's the worst thing that could happen?

GET SOME TRACTION

SELECT GOAL	ACTION	DATE	CHECK WHEN COMPLETE
1.			☐
2.			☐
3.			☐
4.			☐
5.			☐

GET SOME TRACTION

But Wait, There's More

So there I was on a Friday afternoon, in a follow-up interview at a top-ten New York ad agency on Madison Avenue—just like I had envisioned.

And then, breaking a long moment of silence, the head of recruiting for the DDB account executive training program offered me a job paying $24,000 a year! Goal accomplished! Time to celebrate, right?

But, while my mind was saying to take the offer, my gut was telling me to pause. Unlike the others in the program, I had already worked for over a year at an ad agency. I was not "entry level." Didn't I deserve a little more for my experience?

Somewhat to my own shock, I responded, "I'll take $25,000." (Honestly, I hadn't gone in there expecting to negotiate my salary.)

Again, the silence. She just looked at me, her eyes squinting as she sized me up. I quickly added, "I have more experience than the others in the training program."

My head was spinning—*What was I doing?* I just got the job! Oh, my goodness! Maybe it was wrong to trust my gut this time. But now I was stuck, so I tried to calmly stare back, unflinching, waiting for her reply, legs still neatly crossed at the ankles.

Even though I was exhausted (maybe delirious?) from the week of trekking around this "small island," I think, even in that tense moment, I must have been subconsciously calculating, "What is the worst that could happen?" She could have said, "No, we will pay you $24,000." And, well, that's it.

I figured the odds that she would have rescinded the offer entirely at that point were almost zero. Who responds to a candidate who was just offered a position requesting a slightly larger salary coupled with a legitimate rationale with "Get out of my office. You're fired! Wait, never mind. I haven't even officially hired you yet, so just get out!"?

Instead, I saw a slight smile creep over her face. "Okay, Sharon, you have yourself a deal. When can you start?"

Again, "throwing my heart over the bar" changed my mindset, which changed my odds, which changed my outcome.

My last day in New York was a Sunday. While packing, I thought about how I had just landed a job at a top advertising agency in the esteemed account executive training program of DDB in New York City in less than a week, at a slightly higher salary than the standard offer.

I was smiling to myself as I tucked my new $25,000 job offer in my purse, right beside my return plane ticket, my meticulously checked-off appointment book, and my pink paperback about positive thinking.

With plenty of time before the flight, my college friend and soon-to-be Manhattan roommate suggested we attend a new church that she had found in the city, which she thought was pretty cool. *Why not?* I thought. I had a lot to be thankful for after a week like that.

It was Marble Collegiate Church, located on West Twenty-Ninth Street. As we strolled down the sidewalk toward the building's facade, I noticed a statue of a man standing outside the main doors of the church building. "Who's that?" I asked, gesturing up ahead.

"Norman Vincent Peale," she responded. "You know, the guy who wrote that famous book *The Power of Positive Thinking*. This was his church."

CHAPTER 5

If I Can Make It There

Confidence & Calibration

Tell the negative committee that meets inside
your head to sit down and shut up.
—ANN BRADFORD

My Story

And just like that, I was on my way to New York City in a U-Haul truck filled with almost everything I owned, including my cat. I was moving into an apartment over a Chinese restaurant on the Lower East Side of Manhattan. A light snow started to fall when I crossed the Knoxville city limits. While I fumbled to find the wipers on the unfamiliar dashboard, a wave of emotion overtook me. I had been in such a whirlwind of tasks preparing for the trip that there had not been a chance to pause and let it all sink in.

As the snow came down harder, concerning thoughts started bouncing around in my head: *What are you thinking? You hardly know anyone there. You don't belong in New York. You should turn around right now and fix this stupid mistake. You can't make it there!*

Tears welled. I could not believe this! Those voices must have been lurking in the dark for this very moment. The moment when I was all alone and venturing into the unknown. All they needed was the slightest hint of uncertainty from me to unleash every argument against leaving. They were different from the concept of negative self-talk. These voices were accusatory and authoritarian. These silent arguments started with *YOU*, not *I*.

Fortunately, these voices had just made a serious mistake. That last argument of *you can't make it there* redirected my thoughts. It reminded me of the iconic Frank Sinatra song "New York, New York." The lyrics do not downplay that New York City is challenging; it's tough, but it puts a positive spin on the potential to "wake up in a city that never sleeps, and find I'm king of the hill, top of the heap."

Then, as if in response to those voices in my head, while rumbling eastbound on I-40, I belted out the song in solitude: "Start spreading the news. I'm leaving today. I wanna be a part of it, New York, New York." As I continued, I realized that it was almost uncanny how much I needed to hear those very words right at that moment. "These small-town blues are melting away. I'll make a brand-new start of it in old New York."

My confidence was growing as I reached the chorus from this famous ode to New York dreamers. Singing at the top of my lungs over the roaring engine of the U-Haul and the frightened, otherworldly meows of my cat, I went for the big finish: "If I can make it there, I'll make it anywhere. It's up to you, New York, New Yooooooork!" It was not going to be easy, but once again, all I needed was *possible*.

After meeting my future roommate about halfway between Manhattan and Knoxville to help with the driving, we rolled that big U-Haul through the Lincoln Tunnel on Saturday night and moved into our tiny apartment on Sunday. My first day as an assistant account executive trainee at DDB was the following Monday. That morning, I dressed in my new, big-shouldered suit and sneakers—with a nice pair of low pumps in my tote bag. I was on my way, striding with pep and confidence down the New York sidewalk toward the Lexington subway line to head uptown to Forty-Ninth and Madison. Now, *I* was Melanie Griffith in *Working Girl!*

Day one was exhilarating and intimidating all at the exact same time. I had been looking forward to meeting the rest of the participants in the account executive training class, but I did not anticipate how different most of their backgrounds were going to be compared to mine. They were mostly graduates of private and elite schools in the northeast. They included the children of business leaders, oil executives, award-winning authors, US presidential staffers, and people who had surnames you'd likely recognize as descendants of the Gilded Age. I remember jokingly thinking to myself, as this realization sank in, maybe they would just make their own assumptions about who I was … or wasn't. *Oh, of course, Sharon Price, of the T. Rowe Price or Price Waterhouse people?*

I found myself becoming more aware of my accent and trying to avoid Southern colloquialisms. While always truthful, in the beginning, I was understandably conscientious of the socioeconomic differences and would respond to inquiries about my background with carefully crafted comments like "I went to the University of Tennessee because we've lived in the state for several generations, and it's a tradition" (no need to add that I was the first person in my family to get a four-year college degree and I had to pick an in-state school to afford it), and "We don't have a vacation home, but my family does spend time in Florida each year" (no need to mention that we visited the panhandle in a camper, not a condo in Boca Raton).

Despite my redirects, there were certain situations where the realities of our differing financial situations were harder to avoid. My Lower East Side apartment was a fifth-floor walk-up with a kitchen the size of a broom closet and a sitting area where you had to move your feet so someone could walk past to use the bathroom. The aromatic mix of kung pao and chow mein from the restaurant below infused our one shared clothes closet, forcing us to air out our chosen workday ensembles overnight—which did not always work.

In contrast, many of my training program teammates lived in much nicer apartments in more posh areas, often with elevators and doormen, commonly subsidized by their parents. At least some of them were living in their parents' extra condo they kept in the city for the weekend visit every now and then. Welcome to a world where it wasn't uncommon for conversations to nonchalantly include, "Do you want to go to our family ski house/beach house/lake house with us next weekend?"

It seemed to me that most never looked at the prices on the restaurant menu because their credit cards were never on the verge of maxing out, nor did they have to think about things like utility bills, or paying the rent, or sneaking one of those leftover sandwiches or bags of chips from the lunchtime training program presentation into their purse so they could eat dinner that night. In fact, the concern of someone suggesting, "Hey, let's just split the bill," at a big group gathering was always a panic moment for me, since I had probably ordered an appetizer and drank water just to afford to socialize with everyone.

Before I made some friends, I admit that those voices in my head would sometimes interject, *You know the only reason they are inviting you is so someone can say, "Hey, do you want to meet my middle-class friend from Tennessee? Isn't she cute? Say something Southern, Sharon."*

One night, a bunch of us from the training class had agreed to attend an over-the-top event sponsored by any number of big media companies common in that era of the advertising business. Two of the guys who had already graduated from the training program asked if I wanted to join them for a drink beforehand. "We'll stop by the Yale Club for a cocktail, and then head over to the event," they told me.

I smiled and said, "That sounds like a *blast!*"

They were perplexed by my enthusiasm, reminding me that "It's a low-key place." The Yale Club, which you may know, is a private club in Midtown Manhattan, primarily for alumni of the highly esteemed Ivy League school and their guests.

"How can it be low key?" I asked. "Especially with a name like that. I mean, seriously, the *Yell* Club? That's great!"

Both of my friends immediately doubled over with laughter. "Oh my god, Sharon," they howled. "It's the Yaaaaaale Club, not the Yeeeeeeell Club!"

I looked at them, both still laughing out loud in the middle of the sidewalk on Madison Avenue as others passed by glancing our way with curiosity. Maybe I had really blown it this time due to my clear lack of natural assumption that, well, of course, they would be asking me to join them at the *Yaaaale* Club. The voices quickly interjected, *See, you don't belong here at all. Why don't you just give up and go home?* I started to walk away.

Catching his breath, one of the guys added, "Hey, don't you still want to go? It might not be a *blast* but we will make it fun. I promise!" And away we went, arm in arm, to the venerable Yale Club.

You know what? They were just laughing because, well, it was funny. It is important to learn not to overthink someone's comments or add some sort of underlying negative meaning to every situation that could be taken personally when, most of the time, there just isn't any.

Except, on the occasion when there is. I'll never forget attending a gathering that was hosted by a native Bostonian and Harvard grad who reported to me at DDB after I had graduated the training program. When a guest discovered that I was this woman's boss, he was flabbergasted. "Wait a minute," he said, turning to my friend with a sneer. "You mean to tell me that you report to somebody from *Tennessee*?"

The host kicked him out.

Who wants to have their overall worthiness or capability instantaneously judged based on some narrow aspect of their persona? But it was true—my lack of northeastern private school credentials and elite family connections were a reality—and clearly, some people were going to judge and even dismiss me because of that. This quickly became a hot topic for the voices, adding, *How can you possibly think you will ever be successful in New York?*

I recalled a quote from Eleanor Roosevelt, whom I highly respect: "No one can make you feel inferior without your consent." True, but it doesn't mean that is an easy thing to master. Then I was like, *But wait, wasn't she from an elite Manhattan family? Anyway ...*

Clearly, this small island could be tough on your ego, but it was also an energetic roller-coaster ride filled with new experiences, people, places, things, and food! The previous incident aside, I loved it. I could feel the heartbeat of the city and enjoyed my time in Manhattan immensely. My years there were practically nonstop and will always be a part of me.

It was simply exhilarating to work hard and play hard while doing my best to enjoy all the culture and activities the city could offer, even on my limited budget. I learned so much about the advertising industry and business in general, while my cultural experiences and social life also expanded, which included things ranging from absorbing numerous world-class museums to becoming fairly accomplished at talking my way past the storied velvet rope at some of New York's hot spots in the 1990s—which, by the way, is impressive even to a Harvard grad.

In the training program, my first rotation was in the media buying department, where I was asked to audit the magazine advertising placements for one of the most renowned luxury brands in the world, Chanel. Yes, for a short period I was paid to flip through high-end magazines like *Vogue* and *Town & Country* to locate and count Chanel ads. Even though I was doing exactly what I was asked, I questioned if that was really all they wanted. I noticed that sometimes the ad was on the wrong side of the page versus the contract or not on the back cover as specified. All of these advertising placements, or "positions" as they are called, cost different amounts of money based on the estimated number of consumer views, or "impressions." I decided to work after hours on a big box-shaped shared computer that featured a black screen with flashing green type. I used a program called LOTUS 1-2-3 to create a spreadsheet that analyzed the actual page positionings versus what had been ordered to highlight discrepancies and the number of media credits that were due to the client at the end of the quarter. That extra effort contributed to me being promoted nine months ahead of schedule to assistant account executive (no "trainee") to work with the pitch team for a potential new client. Shortly thereafter I was assigned to the esteemed Hershey account.

There were plenty of late nights when I came home exhausted after a long day of writing and rewriting, fact checking, and collating a deck in preparation for an advertising pitch or when I stayed late to complete a detailed conference report. And there were plenty of days that I was convinced this was all a big impossible dream, but I kept working and believing.

Then, after just a few years of expanding responsibilities at DDB, I was recruited by another advertising agency called Backer,

Spielvogel, Bates, to eventually become the account supervisor on the M&M/Mars account, overseeing one of their most important brands with an ad budget of tens of millions of dollars. The position came with a window office in the world-renowned art deco Chrysler Building (Was I "making it there"?) and the opportunity to create a lifelong relationship with one of my mentors, who was the head of the entire account at the time. In this new role, I would be working on the most popular candy bar in the world, Snickers. The 1992 Barcelona Olympic Games were on the horizon, and, as a brand sponsor of the games, we were tasked to develop Snickers' Olympic advertising campaign, working alongside the brand management team at M&M/Mars.

After an important presentation to the client-side top brass, the lead brand manager on Snickers pulled me aside and asked if I had ever considered getting an MBA.

The thought of pursuing an MBA (a master's degree in business administration) had not really crossed my mind, although it was a fairly common next step after a few years of work experience for a lot of ambitious, young businesspeople. My thoughts had been to continue to work my way up in the ad agency business. Yes, I was fascinated by the product development, pricing, sales, strategy, and broader aspects of business on the client side. But an MBA? That was a big—and expensive—step to consider.

"Are you suggesting that I move to Tennessee and go back to school?" I asked him.

He looked back at me like I was nuts, adding, "You could go anywhere, but why don't you stay in the city? Your GMAT scores are still good, right?"

The city? *What* city? Was he really talking about New York City? I should get my MBA in New York? And GMAT scores? I hadn't ever taken the Graduate Management Admissions Test, like so many who have their sights on the business world do their senior year in college. So no, my scores weren't "good." There were no scores.

He continued, almost nonchalantly, "Yeah, apply to Columbia. You shouldn't have any trouble getting in, given your track record."

Columbia University? The Ivy League school established in 1754, with alumni like Warren Buffett, Jack Kerouac, Amelia Earhart, and Alexander Hamilton? This was the college he thought I "shouldn't have any trouble" getting into? What was he talking about?

The idea bounced around my head for days. I got in an argument with the voices. The internal conversation morphed from *You're not nuts, he's nuts,* to *You're underestimating yourself,* from *You can't afford that,* to *Just worry about getting in first,* from *You won't get a good enough score on the GMAT after being out of school this long,* to *You never know until you try.*

Even with my growing ambition and relative success, was it possible that I was selling myself short by not evolving my goals? Maybe I could be or do something that I simply could not have imagined before? But that would take a lot of confidence.

As my head hit the pillow one night after days of back and forth, I remembered a game that my brother invented when I was around five years old. He would place an empty plastic bottle on one end of the living room and tell me, "There are strength pills in there." The goal was to fight my way through this guy who was twice my age and size to get to the pills that would instantly turn me into a superhero. I had to work to reach the prize, and then we would subsequently have an epic pretend "battle."

"Please don't hurt me," he would scream, covering his face with his arms. But with my newfound power, I could take him down without a problem. It always ended with us laughing so hard we cried. *How nice,* I thought, *would it be to have some of those all-powerful "strength pills" right now?*

Then it hit me. I did have them because it was all made up anyway. Strength pills only existed because we believed and agreed that they did. All of us have potential that's only out of reach if we believe it is. My brother wasn't around, but I knew what I needed to do.

Gulp. I got focused. Okay, there's a bit of "fake it till you make it" buried in there, but the idea was to create enough confidence to get me moving toward a potential new goal that I would have deemed completely out of reach before. I just needed enough "super strength" to fight through the first steps. I took a prep course for the GMAT. I took the GMAT. I picked up a Columbia MBA application. I filled it out. I wrote my essays. I asked two very impressive people whom I had worked for at DDB to write my recommendations. I rewrote my essays and waited for my GMAT results to complete my application. Finally, I reread and rewrote my essays yet again. Finished!

> All of us have potential that's only out of reach if we believe it is.

However, before I dropped the manila envelope in the mail, those old annoying voices had something to say about it: *You really think you are going to get into an Ivy League university? Do you know the odds of being accepted to a top-ten MBA program? You don't have enough money to pay the tuition, even if you get in. What are you thinking?*

Yep, the voices were back and on a new mission. And this time they did not make the silly mistake of quoting something that reminded me of an iconic empowering song. Their arguments were honed, professional, and convincing.

This caused me to leave that completed business school application in my tote bag as I went back and forth to work, while I was on subways, riding in taxis, strolling on sidewalks, enjoying dinners, during presentations, and at ad shoots—as the days ticked on. The first-round application deadline passed. The second-round deadline passed. Time was running out.

Then, with one more gulp of strength-pill confidence, in a sheer act of defiance and against the advice from the negative voices, the now tattered envelope that had been carefully addressed and stamped for weeks was hand carried to the Upper West Side to be dropped off at the Columbia Business School admissions office on the last day of the last round.

A Question from the Heart

DO YOU HAVE ENOUGH CONFIDENCE TO PROPERLY CALIBRATE YOUR GOALS?

When I have shared the story of not submitting my Columbia MBA application until the last day of the last round, the assumption could be that I waited because I was arrogant. That I was somehow so confident that I would be accepted that it didn't matter when I turned it in.

On the contrary, I believe it was because I was subconsciously trying to give myself permission to not be accepted. As in, *Well* of course *I didn't get in. I applied on the last day of the last round. What do you expect?*

Merely a few short years before this, attending Columbia was beyond what I could have imagined for myself; therefore, I had calibrated my goals below my new potential possibilities, until someone else challenged my assumptions. Even then, I struggled internally about applying to business school until I mustered up an imaginary boost of self-confidence, thanks to a childhood game my brother invented.

The World Economic Forum published, "Without confidence, much of your competence will go wasted. Build your confidence no matter what the price. The world needs more people that are both confident and competent."[10] Those are strong words with high stakes. Basically, if you cannot build your confidence, you may *never* reach the true potential that your competence could afford.

How do you build confidence? Well, the process of setting and achieving goals is one important tool. However, like it or not, persistent negative thoughts are one of the greatest challenges to building enough confidence to go for your big goals, even if you have already acquired the basic skills associated with the habit of success. Yes, getting control of those annoying voices that run through your mind seeding doubt about your abilities and potential, which may have nothing to do with your actual abilities and potential, could ultimately be the determining factor of you "making it there"—wherever your "there" is—or not.

> If you cannot build your confidence, you may *never* reach the true potential that your competence could afford.

As the opening quote noted, maybe it is time for you to "tell the negative committee that meets inside your head to sit down and shut up." Are you ready?

---

10   Bruce Kasanoff, "Is Confidence More Important Than Competence?" World Economic Forum, March 23, 2015, https://www.weforum.org/agenda/2015/03/is-confidence-more-important-than-competence/.

Without a doubt, taking control of your thinking is key to finding the personal confidence required to achieve your goals. Again, if you can't get those negative voices to shut up, you may not be able to recognize when it could be time to recalibrate your dreams by setting even higher goals—goals that you may not have even imagined for yourself when you first identified your original objectives (for me, like applying to Columbia).

How many applications are you willing to leave in your tote bag?

Now, Create *Your* Story: Fire Your Negative Committee!

Although the negative committee voices in our heads are normal to some degree, they are also the enemy of confidence. In study after study, *confidence* has been proven to be a more predictive factor of success than *competence*. That's right, I will state it again: having *confidence* in your ability to do something is just as, and sometimes more, important than having the *competence* to do it. And without *confidence*, you may never correctly *calibrate* your goals to your actual potential.

Thus far, I have shared some techniques to keep self-doubt at bay, including doing gut checks, using logic (like asking yourself, *What's the worst thing that can happen?*), and maybe even finding your own version of my brother's silly strength-pill game.

However, there are times when the persistence of the negative committee is so overwhelming, and the arguments are so convincing, that the typical approaches don't work. The committee chatter can literally keep you up at night! This is because they are very good at using a practical kind of argument that is based in so-called facts grounded in your own self-doubts and fears, including *It is time to be practical and face reality,* or *No one from your family/town/background has ever achieved a dream like that.*

They are particularly good at throwing these arguments at you during a weak moment or a setback. Trust me, this negative committee is formidable and has derailed many a goal or dream, even some of my own.

However, just like anyone or any group who is purposefully working against or undermining the stated goals of an organization (in this case, *you*), the actions of the negative committee need to be addressed, and it seems to me there are clear grounds for them to be permanently dismissed! Here's how:

- Ask your negative committee to provide a memo covering all the goals that you can't accomplish or shouldn't try and why. Tell them to get it all out, no matter how ugly, because you expect a full report concerning your ridiculous dreams and innate shortfalls. (Of course, you will have to write this memo on their behalf.)

- Read the memo from the negative committee out loud. (Warning: this could be emotional.)

- Tell the negative committee (again, out loud) that they are wrong and not in charge of your life. *You* are. You are their boss. Not the other way around. Yell this if it makes you feel good and then *fire* the negative committee for their blatant incompetence, lack of vision, and misrepresentation of the truth!

Now, take the info from the memo and translate all of their negative points about what you can't do and why into positive points about what you can do and why. Then, have a little fun and dispose of that ridiculous lie-filled negative committee memo. How? Shred it? Burn it? Tear it into tiny pieces and throw it out of a helicopter? Bury it in the backyard? Whatever you do, make it memorable. And do it with *confidence*.

MEMO FROM THE NEGATIVE COMMITTEE

Date:

To: You

From: Your Negative Committee

Subject: Things You Can't Do!

Dear You,

We want to remind you of the things you can't do and why. You can't achieve your goals and dreams! Be reasonable! Here's our assessment of what you can't do and why:

- _____
- _____
- _____
- _____
- _____
- _____

By the way, who do you think you are?

Signed,

Your Negative Committee

Date:

To: You

From: Your Negative Committee

Subject: Things You Can't Do!

REJECTED

The Positive Committee Restatements

- _____
- _____
- _____
- _____
- _____

Repeat daily.

But Wait, There's More

When the acceptance letter for Columbia arrived, I was shocked and thrilled—and a little scared. Even so, within a few months, I was moving to the Upper West Side into a studio apartment right off Broadway, walking distance to Columbia University's campus.

Take it from me, strength pills work. I mean, they don't *really* work. Or do they? Well, if the strength pills squelched the negative committee long enough for me to find the confidence to apply to Columbia, I could argue that they did indeed work. Even if it was just all in my head, that's okay. The negative committee voices that are impacting our self-confidence and keeping us from going after our goals are also *just in our head*. Aren't they?

Fair warning, after you go through the process outlined above to write and destroy a memo from your negative committee, they can still eventually regroup, and you need to recognize them and be prepared. It may seem like they are just trying to *protect* you from disappointment, but left unchecked they can become much more sinister and damaging. And sometimes, they may need more attention to be properly managed than you can muster on your own. In these cases, it's important to seek support.

My handsome, funny, smart big brother, who apparently had an innate instinct to make sure his little sister was in touch with her inner superhero, died at only forty-nine years old. He had been struggling with his own negative voices. He had bargained with everyone not to tell his little sister about his challenges with alcohol because he was so concerned how heartbroken I would be. He was right.

After his death, I realized that I had not thanked him for helping me find my inner power all those years ago. Now I would never be able to return the favor because, I guess, sometimes there just aren't enough strength pills.

CHAPTER 6

Pick Your Path

Straight or Scenic?

Roads were made for journeys not destinations.
−CONFUCIUS

The Story

On the morning of my first day back at school, the sixteen-block walk from my new apartment to the same place I had submitted my application months earlier provided plenty of time to contemplate. Upon entering the iron gates of Columbia University's beautiful and storied Manhattan campus, I thought, *Wow, this is a chance of a lifetime!* followed quickly by, *Am I really giving up two years of income and paying* tens of thousands of dollars *to go* back *to school?*

Obviously, I had rationalized this concern already, but it resurfaced with a punch when an older super-practical work buddy told me that you really learn only two things in business school: "More money is better than less money" and "Money now is better than money later." That's it. Now you know. So why go? According to him,

I was already "failing" because with my first tuition check, I had a lot *less money—now.*

My plan quickly became to maximize my educational experience while focusing on getting my degree as efficiently as possible. Separately, because Columbia has a finance-focused, *quantitative* program, it should supplement my already strong *qualitative* skill set. That's valuable, right?

Even though I was lugging a heavy early-generation laptop computer in my backpack, with that concerning thought swimming in my head, it's even more understandable why breathing became difficult as I climbed the stairs to the business school's main building, Uris Hall. I paused as others pushed and hustled around me to enter the glass doors. Could I really do this?

By now, unknown waters were not foreign to me. But this time, I knew that I was not just on the precipice of jumping into a different pool; I was flinging myself into the academic deep end without a float. Everything seemed to shift to slow motion as a memory from childhood flooded my mind.

On a hot summer day, I stood alone on the wobbly high board overlooking the twelve-foot section of the pool at our local recreation center. I was proudly sporting my stars-and-stripes swimsuit, with my dad in the water far below; he urged me to take the big leap. Kids were lining up, standing on the tall ladder behind me, waiting for their turn to jump. I just *had* to do it. Chickening out now would force me to walk back across the diving board and ask everyone to climb down so I could make an embarrassing exit. Still scared, I took a deep breath and leaped through the air like a patriotic superhero until—*splash!* I was underwater. Once oriented, I could just make out the blurry image of Daddy smiling above the surface, and I began swimming toward him. *Wow, that was fun!*

Once again, I was awash with the reinforcing comfort of being reminded that most of the time when I have been afraid of something but did it anyway, it was more than likely to be a great experience rather than a bad one. I smiled, inhaled deeply, entered the main door, and launched myself right into the foreign waters of the Ivy League educational waters. There was no turning back.

At the incoming student orientation, there was no commentary about looking to the left and looking to the right with only one of us expected to graduate. On the contrary, we were reminded of some esteemed alumni, including well-known billionaires, investment gurus, CFOs, and CEOs. I even recall hearing that someone in our class had received a *perfect* score on their GMAT. (It wasn't me.) Nope, I was definitely no longer in the *shallow end*.

My first core class of the semester was accounting. After surveying the room full of mostly guys (women only comprised about 15 percent of my class), I found a seat near the back. The professor was moving through the information quickly. I dug out my syllabus and studied it. Had there been some prereading or prework? Nothing.

At a break, I leaned over to a classmate and asked why everyone seemed to be picking up these topics so quickly. Was I missing something? Was I drowning already?

"Well, a lot of these guys are already certified public accountants," he whispered.

Okey dokey. I hadn't taken so much as a single accounting class in my life. Wasn't that why we were there? To learn? What were a bunch of actual accountants doing in an entry-level accounting class? I was excited about my steep-learning-curve theory, but this was more like *extreme learning*. I felt automatically way *behind* the curve—maybe even underwater with no blurry image of someone who could save me swimming on the surface, just in case.

WARNING: Embarrassingly Naive Question Ahead! After absorbing the revelation that the first semester accounting class was filled with a bunch of actual CPAs, I leaned over again and asked, "Why are they taking the class if they already know the material?"

He looked straight ahead and without a hint of sarcasm flatly added, "To get a better GPA."

Frankly, I shouldn't have been surprised. Yes, your grade point average (GPA) is important. It's one of the ways the top companies choose graduates for their best jobs. A tenth of a point on your GPA could determine if you get selected for the number one management consulting firm versus the number two management consulting firm. Although Columbia had tried to manage the situation with a more generalized grading approach, it still mattered. Securing these job positions is incredibly competitive (and lucrative), and you're not just competing with other graduates at Columbia but with MBA candidates at other top programs. My I-can't-wait-to-learn-all-of-this-new-stuff self just swallowed a little sobering reality that seemed simultaneously so obvious and so disheartening. Here I was, believing my goal was to maximize my educational "return on investment" by *learning* as much as I could, while they were more focused on getting a great GPA and *earning* as much as they could. I know some of the guys from my Columbia graduation class are laughing at me right now about how ridiculous my idea was, but maybe I just had a different idea about what mattered to me and I didn't even know it yet.

Like I said, Columbia Business School is known for quantitative disciplines like finance and economics, so the halls were, and still are, filled with very bright people who innately excel at linear thinking. Although comfortable in these disciplines, because I am naturally more of a communicator and creative, I tended to think differently than a lot of the others in the program. I recall needing to try to translate some of my holistic thought processes into sequential arguments before I would speak. Little did I know it, but learning how to do that, plus being exposed to the "language of business," would be some of my most valuable lessons. Mastering the ability to contemplate and communicate in both a holistic *and* analytical manner allowed me to *see* and tackle problems from different perspectives. I was developing a more balanced left-brained/right-brained thinking process (called "transcontextual" thinking), which can be very valuable for problem solving, especially in multidimensional situations—like being a CEO.

This unlock was most useful during the infamous business school case studies. Cases are where you and other classmates team up to read about a business situation, decision, or problem that a certain company has faced. The goal is to present the best solution or next step based on the data provided. For a team to crush a case requires both linear and nonlinear/holistic thinking. Spreadsheets, situation assessments, potential strategies, and compelling arguments require both hard *and* soft skills. There's always a real outcome, which is what the company actually ended up doing, but the point is more about how the teams work together to tackle the problem and present a logic chain and argument that supports their answer. So even though I was a little *underwater* in some swim lanes in the beginning, I discovered that I was already a strong swimmer in others, although I had not valued those skills as much—maybe *because* they came easier to me.

Shortly after I got comfortable in my new environment, an announcement was made about the international exchange program that sounded interesting to me. Seriously? Just after discovering I could swim in the academic deep end after all, was I really going to contemplate a move overseas that would put me in even more debt? I was almost frustrated with myself for even considering it! I didn't think I had a chance because only a dozen students or so were selected, but in a testing-fate kinda way, I applied.

And then I was accepted to the program! Now what? Did I really want to get off this very clear, exactly what I had planned, straight path to getting my MBA as efficiently as possible and move to another country? Thanks, *fate*.

Before the semester was over, I said, "Goodbye, straight path" and "Hello, scenic road." The historic Katholieke Universiteit Leuven (the Catholic University of Leuven), which was founded in 1425, is located a short train ride east of Brussels, Belgium. The mid-1990s was a fascinating time to be in Europe, particularly in Belgium, because the seat of the future European Union (EU) was in Brussels, and some of the international business professors who would be teaching the classes in Leuven were part of the consortium leading the creation of the EU and the contemplation of the creation of the euro. I jumped right into the Leuven student life by renting a one-room flat and making the necessary purchase of a classic bicycle—the ubiquitous way to get around this age-old college town.

While there, I was also determined to stick to my goal of maximizing my educational ROI by being on a train exploring someplace new as often as possible. All I needed was a backpack, a good pair of shoes, a map, and a Europass for discounted train travel—plus an occasional travel buddy!

Brussels, Rome, Munich, Amsterdam, Paris, Barcelona, Madrid—I crisscrossed the continent with an adventure-filled itinerary that included obligatory things like art museums, cathedrals, and classic landmarks, but also purposefully included *nontouristy* sidetracks to smaller towns and cities. From the North Sea to the Strait of Gibraltar, I met wonderful people who shared their stories and culture with me. My schoolwork took precedence, of course, even though I may have faxed it from a local post office on occasion, if I couldn't get back in time for class, given this was in the days before the internet, email, or smart phones were common. This scenic route experience exposed me to many different and unexpected things, placing me in situations where I was constantly taking calculated risks to the point that it felt natural to do so. And I loved it.

It is important to note, however, that choosing the less predictable, more unusual, maybe even rougher road because you think it's something you *should do* versus something you *want to do* is not the goal. Life is *not* supposed to be "hard for hard's sake." It's supposed to be challenging, so you can grow and learn. It should be winding, so you can enjoy the view. It's intended to be interesting, so you can cultivate wonderful memories.

You might be questioning how to tell the difference between these roads. The answer is by the way you *feel*. What? Yes, while navigating a less traveled, more scenic road will require extra exertion no matter why you may have chosen to take it, the *wrong* path just feels exhausting, while the *right* path feels exciting.

In either case, no unknowns, no pressure, no evolution, no learning, no growth. That's just the way it is—it's a universal law. So since

> Life is *not* supposed to be "hard for hard's sake." It's supposed to be challenging, so you can grow and learn. It should be winding, so you can enjoy the view.

the unknown is really unavoidable anyway, the real question is this: Do you wait for an inevitable challenging road to be randomly thrust upon you, or do you choose to strategically divert from the straight path from time to time to purposefully experience the less traveled, scenic route that then becomes the impetus for faster further personal evolution?

I noticed this construct of contemplating, questioning, and creating ways to constantly evolve was seeping both into my life and into my studies. In one of my marketing classes in Leuven we were competing against a computer program in a simulated market share battle. Our team did well by playing the game the *right* way given the program parameters. However, I wrote a supplemental paper making the argument that if all one does is follow the most obvious implied action of the data, in a real-life competitive environment this it will often lead to an inferior decision because you are likely to replicate the same strategy as your competitors, who presumably have access to the same data.

I postulated that the real way to win is by occasionally doing something unexpected or unpredictable. To do this in a strategic way requires an ability and willingness to first study the data and identify the norm and then, with full knowledge, purposefully defy the obvious next step enough to assure you are creating a unique tactic or positioning. That takes courage, but if you are willing to zag when the rest of the word is likely to zig, that's when opportunity shows up.

As business school graduation drew closer, a concern was looming in the back of my mind. Although much more lucrative (and obviously more aligned with ROI, based on *earning* versus *learning*), the idea of taking a job in industries often preferred by Columbia MBAs, like investment banking, private equity, management consulting, or venture capital, would not be something that I truly *loved*.

I was drawn to more marketing-centric, consumer-facing businesses. Maybe it was time to embrace that I was naturally more of a creative, who also happened to think analytically, instead of trying to become something or someone else by ignoring or devaluing my creative side. Maybe what made me different at business school was not a weakness but my secret superhero power and what I really needed to do was jump off the proverbial high board (again) and embrace it.

A Question from the Heart

DO YOU WANT TO TAKE THE STRAIGHT OR SCENIC ROUTE?

Drive and focus are considered bellwethers of success, but sometimes tenacious goal orientation can cause us to completely ignore broader opportunities for growth. Despite the achievement often associated with the most efficient route, much of the joy in life comes from the learning and experiences gained when we ditch our best-laid plans to explore the possibilities found only on the scenic route.

A professor at Columbia Business School noted in *Fast Company* that while research has shown goal setting to be great, it can also lead to undesirable behaviors and unintended consequences.[11] Something coined as "extreme goal setting" is said to

> Much of the joy in life comes from the learning and experiences gained when we ditch our best-laid plans to explore the possibilities found only on the scenic route.

kill creativity and perpetuate a fixed mindset versus a growth mindset. The article adds that "it is important to recognize what motivates us … and what we enjoy the most, because we tend to give our best when we are satisfied and happy." Therefore, "as much as setting rigid goals gives us a sense of security, real growth comes from being able to handle and manage randomness."

If you are thinking about how much time you spent on your Goal Tree for me to now tell you to just forget about it, that's not exactly

---

11   Stephanie Vozza, "Why Setting Goals Can Actually Make You Less Successful," *Fast Company*, February 7, 2017, https://www.fastcompany.com/3067813/why-setting-goals-can-actually-make-you-less-successful.

the case. It's simply important to realize that you should not get so focused on what you think you are *supposed* to be doing—due to goals written based in your current limited knowledge—that you miss out on what you are *meant* to be doing. Things change. You change. So goals can change too.

The truth is, no one really knows how things come together or why things happen a certain way. But there is a beauty, almost a peace, in that perhaps we are all meant to be doing something special with our lives, planned or unplanned. And if you can believe that any kind of infinite wisdom exists, then you can also imagine that you don't know everything. If you don't know everything, then the best you can do is set your goals, walk your path, and keep your mind and your heart open to different potential life "routes" if and when they present themselves. Baseball great Yogi Berra said, "When you come to a fork in the road, take it." Which fork will *you* take?

Now, Create *Your* Story: Plan Some Serendipity!

My early penchant for being goal oriented caused my mom to occasionally say, "Stop wishing your life away." She was concerned that I was so focused on getting from point A to point B that I didn't look around to see what was between the "points," *which is not the "point."*

To be clear, learning to set and achieve goals is part of the journey, but not the *point* of the journey. I believe my life has been more fun and interesting, while perhaps surprisingly also leading me on a path to reach goals well beyond what I could have seen for myself because I have occasionally taken the "scenic route."

It is okay to develop your peripheral vision for life. You never know what might catch your attention and lead you in a different direction that opens a door that you couldn't have possibly imagined. A few turns off the straight path or a couple of miles on a dirt road is not a bad thing, a waste of time, nor a proof point of your imminent failure. These moments of exploration can be life changing in very positive ways. Enjoy the serendipity of your journey. Better yet, learn to *create* some serendipity in your journey.

Yes, that idea seems like an oxymoron. How can you plan for something that, by definition, is supposed to be by chance? Well, the cofounders of the company Get Satisfaction refer to it as "planned serendipity." They note that routine is the "enemy of serendipity," so the key is to consciously break your routine.[12] When you purposely put yourself in unfamiliar situations or engage with new people with different ideas, you increase your odds of planned serendipity.

Think about what you can do to shake up your routine—starting tomorrow! Now that your Goal Tree and your One Hundred Wishes list represent general destinations, it can be uncanny how things start to present themselves. Way leads to way, and then you meet someone who has just the right info for you to get to the next branch on your tree *or* presents an exciting option to climb out on a new branch that you had never considered.

While you are on your serendipity exploration, note that changing your environment is just a *trick* to raise your level of awareness. Repetition and routine can make us *unconscious*, causing us to miss insights and possibilities. Putting yourself in new environments helps to break that tendency. The real key is to become more *conscious* and appreciative every day, even in the mundane. In the meantime, why not give serendipity a fighting chance by shaking up your regular activities or routine? Who knows what path it might lead to? Here's some starter

---

12   Ned Smith, "Good Luck in Business Is Hard Work," Business News Daily, May 29, 2012, https://www.businessnewsdaily.com/2592-luck-role-business-success.html.

ideas, but please feel free to add your own:

- Sign up for some volunteer work.

- Learn a new skill/take a course/start a hobby.

- Go on a trip or a vacation to a place you have never been—by yourself.

- Choose something from your One Hundred Wishes list and get to it!

SERENDIPITY STARTERS

1. _____
2. _____
3. _____
4. _____
5. _____
6. _____
7. _____
8. _____
9. _____
10. _____

But Wait, There's More

With graduation only a few weeks away, it became clear that I was going to need to get off the straight path, again, and create my own job search strategy. After some introspection and research, I identified a wish list of a few iconic, branded, consumer-facing companies to contact for potential interviews.

At the time, three of the companies were headquartered in the Los Angeles area, so I used a page from my old playbook. I secured a flight to LA before calling each company to tell them I would "be in the area soon," and I asked if I could stop by for an interview.

This time, there was no need to convince someone to walk my résumé to HR, as I quickly arranged the meetings with the first two companies. However, the last one, which had emerged as my top choice, had not called me back. It was Mattel Toys.

Mattel is a kid-centric company known for creativity and innovation and it didn't hurt that their headquarters is in El Segundo, California, a coastal city right next to the Pacific Ocean. Any of the nearby beautiful beach cities would be a wonderful place to live and a short commute away. Plus, the iconic Mattel doll, Barbie, was one of my favorite toys when I was a little girl!

As my flight date drew closer, I struggled with whether it was a good idea to call Mattel to inquire why they had not gotten back to me about my upcoming trip to LA. I had two other interviews with awesome organizations. But I couldn't shake it. It was just plain confusing. I kept thinking about how my branding and advertising background should fit so well at the company—and how much fun it must be to work there.

Less than a week before the flight, I broke down and called Mattel's HR department. I told them it was because I wanted to understand why they hadn't called, so I could improve my résumé. They put me on hold for quite a while. My heart raced as I listened to the loop of recorded Barbie songs.

Finally, a nice gentleman got on the phone. "We found your résumé. What position were you looking for again?"

"To work in product management and marketing, preferably on the Barbie business," I responded.

He said matter-of-factly, "Oh … well, your background is perfect for that."

Confused, I replied (not believing this came out of my mouth), "I know."

"But you'll have an MBA from Columbia," he continued.

For lack of a better response, I repeated, "I know," pausing and then quickly adding, "but my goal is to work in product management and marketing, preferably on Barbie."

He added somberly, "Well, someone had put your résumé in the finance pile because of your Columbia MBA, and there's no opening there." Just as I was about to thank him and hang up, his tone became completely different as he added, "But of course, we would love to talk to you about product management." With that, Mattel was added to my LA agenda!

The offer came just in time. My funds had dwindled down to a few dollars. I was living on boxed mac and cheese and had nearly maxed out one of my credit cards while the other had been canceled. At that point, I couldn't even justify the purchase of the light-blue cap and gown to take part in the grand commencement on Columbia's beautiful green, where the famous *Alma Mater* statue's outstretched arms seemingly offer a blessing to those who have achieved this impressive token of academic accomplishment. (That makes me sad to this day.) Even so, I watched from the sidelines, filled with pride and gratefulness for this school and this experience, as the fresh crop of grads tossed their mortarboards into the air on a spring day in 1994.

To be clear, my compensation package at Mattel paled in comparison to those in the class who took a more traditional path or attained one of those top management consulting jobs, including some of those guys in my first accounting class.

In retrospect, you could argue that I never really understood "the two things you learn at business school" because I was choosing to make less money over a job that would pay more money, and I was gambling on making "money later" versus making "money now." So clearly, I was not achieving my goal of getting the best possible ROI for graduating from this renowned institution.

Or maybe, I was already starting to innately define what success meant to me. What was this *ROI* I was going for anyway? What kind of *return* was I looking for? How much money is a wonderful experience worth? How much value would there be in looking back on my life and saying, "Wow, that was a blast"? What is the price of happiness?

A few weeks later, I packed everything I could fit in my old blue Mazda that had been sitting in my parents' garage since I left for New York five years earlier. I was $60,000 in college debt with nothing in LA but a belief that Mattel was the perfect place for me.

A dear friend from my advertising days agreed to join me on the cross-county car trip. In a fitting manner, we did not feel obligated to stick to the most efficient route. We hiked the Grand Canyon, visited Four Corners, enjoyed the Navajo Nation, explored the ancient Anasazi ruins, and, for a while there, were on a dirt road that was not even on the map.

That first Christmas after starting my new job, I flew to Tennessee to see my family. On the way back to LA, instead of a direct flight, I stopped in Chicago to visit a friend for New Year's Eve, whom I had met during my European exchange at KU Leuven through a similar program at the University of Chicago.

While there, we were joking around about my new dating philosophy that I had created since the move to LA. Because of the blessing of contrast provided during my years in New York, I was now completely clear about what I *did not* want in a future partner. To be clear, I've never felt like I always needed to be dating somebody and, having recently turned thirty years old, even decided it would be fine if I never found "the one." But to improve my odds (just in case), I playfully wrote a long list of attributes I thought I *did* want in a husband.

Top of the list—his first name could not be *John*. I had dated a long string of *Johns*, and nothing against these guys, but I simply thought it was time to move on, at least to a new name. My friend thought this whole idea was hilarious, which, admittedly, it was.

Later that evening while at a popular gathering place near the University of Chicago, two other Chicago MBAs joined our table. My friend, much to my surprise and horror, started nonchalantly grilling the guys on my newly created "husband checklist"—unbeknownst to them, thank goodness. Amazingly, one of the guys was nearly a perfect fit. For example, among many other random things, he was at least thirty years old (having just celebrated his thirtieth birthday a few weeks earlier), had grown up in a small town, and liked sports. Plus, his first name was *not* John—it was Russ.

Toward the end of the evening, my friend shared that she was looking for a position in management consulting, and this guy, who worked at one of the larger firms, offered to help her. They exchanged numbers. When she called him later that week, he asked her for *my* number.

He was coming to LA to pitch a potential new client for his management consulting company and decided to ask me out on a date. I said no. I did not want a long-distance relationship, and he lived in Cleveland. (By the way, he had also been on a layover in Chicago for New Year's on his way back to his home after visiting his parents in Nebraska for the holidays.)

Before hanging up, he caught me off guard by challenging me with my own words: "What's the worst thing that could happen? At least you'll have a nice dinner and a great story to tell someday."

I had to smile and agreed. When he told me his full name was Russ *John*, I almost fell off my chair. What was I going to do now, without sounding totally insane? I couldn't possibly renege because his last name was *John* and that I had this crazy list and ... well, no way. Besides, my criterion was that his *first name* could not be *John*. Maybe it would be okay.

To make a long story short, I married that guy. A guy I met because I was visiting someone associated with an unplanned international exchange program, in conjunction with a school I'd never dreamed of going to, while headed back to a city where I had to make a flyer call just to secure an interview a few months before, on a forty-eight-hour layover side trip for both of us, shortly after making a list specifically outlining the type of guy that I wanted to marry. Planned serendipity?

Over twenty-five years and three kids later, we are still on the scenic route.

CHAPTER 7

Perfectly Pink

Perfectionism & Empowerment

And now that you don't have to be perfect, you can be good.
—JOHN STEINBECK

My Story

Welcome to the *other* Manhattan, a seaside town called Manhattan Beach, located in the land of palm trees and perfection. Admittedly, it was a welcome change after the cold, dirty slush endured during my last winter in New York. However, I had not yet completely grasped how different the LA Barbie-girl vibe was going to be from the buttoned-down Columbia Business School vibe.

Being a new assistant product manager in the Fashions division of the Barbie brand was a childhood dream come true. And no, that's not hyperbole. As a kid and into my teenage years, becoming a fashion designer was my dream career until interior design and architecture took over.

My mom and grandmother taught me how to sew, and one summer afternoon Mom allowed me to host a Barbie fashion design contest at our house for the girls in my neighborhood, followed by a doll fashion show. She generously offered all of her extra fabric remnants and sewing stuff for us to use in our design endeavors. My Barbies and my collection of Dawn dolls—a smaller-stature fashion doll that was popular in the 1970s—were more than just toys to me. They were conduits for storytelling. Like many children, I wove relationships between the characters and took them on many adventures. It was creative and fun.

Mattel, the largest toy manufacturer in the world at the time, was started in 1945. One of the founders was Ruth Handler, an extraordinary woman who is credited for launching Barbie in 1959, which is one of the best-selling toy brands in history. By the time I started, she had already retired, but I was so fortunate to have met her at a special event during my tenure.

From Barbie's introduction through most of my childhood, the brand was hugely popular. But in the '70s and '80s, Barbie had lost momentum with sales having significantly declined from their heyday by the late '80s.

However, by the time I came on board, Barbie had recently had a resurgence, reenergized with new girl-empowerment positioning. And by 1996, Barbie's billion-plus dollars in annual sales represented a significant portion of the company's total revenue.

I was mesmerized with it all. After receiving my corporate access badge sporting my photo and Mattel's iconic red-dot logo on my first day, I was ready to learn. When I started my new job, *every single person* (except for the CEO) in my direct-report structure was a woman, representing about seven layers. That's pretty remarkable even in today's world for a company that size, but back in the midnineties, it was truly rarified air.

But why not? Literally, the most important brand at the company was created by a woman, and the brand's tagline was "We girls can do anything!"

The Barbie brand was a cultural icon and a marketing powerhouse, and I was a part of it all! It was an exhilarating time. And yet, something did not feel right. It wasn't exactly cultural, like being a Southerner in the northeast (I knew what that felt like) or being a creative thinker in a quantitative environment (I knew what that felt like too). It was something more elusive. I thought maybe it was the East Coast/West Coast thing, but it started to become apparent that I was surrounded by women who seemed to me to be, well, *perfect*.

One of these many amazing people whom you couldn't help but admire was the woman who had revived Barbie in the '90s, Jill Barad. She had risen to the level of chief operating officer by the time I started and was one of those many women in my report structure. In 1994, *People* magazine selected her as one of the "50 Most Beautiful People in the World" and put her on their cover. And a few years later, she became one of just four women CEOs of a Fortune 500 company. Jill was driven and inspiring. She had a keen instinct, especially about marketing, and I enjoyed learning from her. But let's be honest: when the *boss* has both smashed the glass ceiling *and* is one of the world's most beautiful people, well …

Every day, the alarm clock welcomed me to the land where the sun seemed to always shine, and I went to work for a brand known for perfection, which was run by what I perceived to be a whole lot of arguably perfect women.

I watched and absorbed. Executive presence. Executive reverence. Corporate culture. Fashion knowledge. Brand history and the all-important innate understanding of what Barbie (the *person*, if she were real) would or would not *do* or *wear*.

I also learned that not only were the right clothes, jewelry, and hair important for Barbie; they were critical for the stewards of the brand, as well. Remember, one of my jobs had been assessing ad placements in high-end fashion magazines, so I knew a Chanel suit when I saw one. Therefore, you can trust me when I tell you that my closet was truly lacking, especially since I was paying back all those student loans from getting my MBA at Columbia.

Even with my admittedly suboptimal wardrobe, I remained focused on acclimating. I learned that there was a bit of a pecking order as to when to speak, especially on the design side, where the responses were more often opinion driven. Without knowing all the history of "why" we had or had not done this or that (like when to avoid yellow shoes or add more glitter), I decided to be cautious and keep my opinions close to my (nondesigner) vest. When an idea or question occurred to me during a meeting, I just figured that it had already been thought of or asked before. How could my idea be so unique? But with that attitude, before I knew it, without really intending, I hadn't said much of anything for months. And that's what happens when you are worried about making sure whatever you are planning to say is *perfect* before you say it.

Where was this insecurity coming from? Clearly, some seeds of perfectionism could have been planted years ago from the cheer, dance, and gymnastics culture that I grew up around. It is a very real thing that you lose points on your bars, beam, vault, or floor routines if your toes aren't pointed or if you didn't stick the landing.

Just when I needed it most, a senior executive on the Barbie team, whom I respected greatly, pulled me aside to share a harsh dose of reality.

"Sharon," she said, "why aren't you contributing in the meetings? I can tell the wheels are turning in your head, but you aren't adding anything."

I explained how important it was to me to learn as much as I could before speaking. I didn't want to say anything unless I was certain it would be beneficial.

"We're not paying you to just sit there," the senior executive told me. "We're paying you to create value for this brand and this company. You are a part of this team now, and we expect you to contribute. Do you understand that?"

Ouch. But it was exactly what I needed to hear. Little did she realize that she had unleashed something deep within me. She'd basically *ordered* me to be myself. They actually wanted to hear what I had to say. More than that, she'd told me that I wasn't fighting for my place at the Mattel table. I didn't need permission to be in the Barbie Club—I was already a member. I was already perfectly perfect, just the way I was.

The next five years at Mattel were a complete blast. I tackled my Barbie Fashions assignment like it was the most important piece of business at the company, even though it was a tiny and declining segment compared to the almighty dolls.

Over the previous several years, the fashion "play pattern," as we called it, had shifted. Barbie was no longer as much about changing the doll's clothes like it was in the 1960s and '70s. It was about playing out the marketing positioning of each individual doll—like, say, flying around the Butterfly Princess Barbie in your backyard or pretending Veterinarian Barbie was helping little plastic puppy and kitty patients. Basically, Barbie Fashions had fallen out of fashion.

From working hand in hand with the designers and developers, to visiting factories in Asia, to personally restocking Barbie Fashions at the local Toys 'R' Us, I wanted to learn everything I could about the consumers, the business, and the supply chain. My hope was that these efforts would lead to insights as to how we could improve the marketing, product, margin, or process. However, it was a meeting early in my assignment that created a real spark. The team and I were discussing how big we thought our business segment could be. In other words, what were the business unit goals? They told me that Barbie Fashions was already about 98 percent of the eleven-and-a-half-inch doll fashion business, so there really wasn't that much room to grow. Hmmm. To me that was like saying, "Even though you might be somebody in this town, this town is small, so I guess you are pretty much done." They had not changed their perspective yet.

"Okay," I said. "But how big is the business as a percentage of discretionary income spent on products around five-dollar retail for little girls?"

That perspective shift helped us think about competition and opportunity differently. In business terms, this is called changing the "competitive realm." Simply put, in business and life, when we start to outgrow our competition—or town, or stadium section—it is time to redefine it.

Even more critical than the limited competitive-realm thinking was the fact that the current fashion assortments looked nothing like the Barbie Fashions I'd loved as a child. In my opinion, the line had been cost reduced so much that the details and accessories that made playing with the fashions really fun in the first place had mostly been removed.

> Simply put, in business and life, when we start to outgrow our competition—or town, or stadium section—it is time to redefine it.

There was also a strong point of view that the retail price that consumers would pay for a single Barbie Fashion was capped at around five dollars, so we could not add back the details without destroying the margin or pricing ourselves out of the market. However, it seemed to me that if the play value was there, we could raise the price and the consumer demand would follow. (Was that price/value equation class paying off again?)

In an ironic twist, because the Fashions business was so comparatively *unimportant*, I was able to have more influence and latitude on a project than *typical* for someone at my level. We pulled together to pitch a concept that led to the development and introduction of a new assortment of fashions that added back a lot of the details from the past, including hose, purses, and shoes, while defying the previously held price point parameters and presented it to the retail trade. We called the line "Fashion Avenue." It worked, and we doubled the Barbie Fashions business the next year.

Separately, after seeing research noting how many Barbie dolls were given as gifts, we developed a new concept called Barbie Fashion Greeting Cards as the perfect add-on purchase, which we merchandised in the toy aisle on something called a clip-strip. This card, with an attached Barbie Fashion, was an easy "grab and go" plus-up when buying a doll—it worked too.

With these two successes, my responsibilities expanded to include a division of Barbie *dolls* and the oversight of the Barbie section for the most important event of the year: the upcoming New York Toy Fair. Millions of dollars were invested to entice retail buyers from around the country to get excited about the newest toy innovations at NYTF. Floors of themed rooms were filled with staging, props, screens, music, actors, and pageantry, all in the hope of securing big holiday orders. The Barbie area was known for its plush pink carpet and a succession of areas featuring key dolls that were often elaborately tricked out. There could be last-minute requests from the executives, and it was not unusual to work all night to assure that we were completely ready for a big customer early the next morning.

Initiative and dedication were highly regarded and could earn you opportunities like getting to join Jill and a group of Mattel's top executives along with Tom Hanks on a tour through the exhibit after hours. Seriously, when we got to the *Toy Story* section (Mattel had the toy license for the film at the time), Tom stepped behind the actor playing the part of Woody the Cowboy and recited portions of Woody's dialogue from the beloved movie while moving the actor's arms with the actor mouthing along.

Amazing, yes, but this kind of magical thing is not that unusual in the toy business. The industry is fast paced, fun, creative, entertaining, and right up my alley. In the coming years, I continued to push the envelope and earn assignments to more challenging areas.

One of the things I learned about marketing and branding at Mattel that I still use today is that *everything* communicates—even if you leave the back of the doll box blank, that is *saying* something. Just like when I wasn't speaking in meetings, it was still *saying* something. However, after I understood that my comments or questions *did not need to be perfect*—I became empowered. That sense of empowerment to more freely ask questions or share ideas was also saying something—and that led to me being able to contribute to the creation of value for the company and being promoted six times over the next five years.

 ## A Question from the Heart

IS THE PURSUIT OF PERFECTIONISM KEEPING YOU FROM BEING EMPOWERED?

Sadly, being a perfectionist has cleverly positioned itself as a badge of honor wrapped in the facade of achieving your best self, when it's the opposite. It is a dangerous and unachievable quest that undermines the ambitions of countless talented people.

The knock-on danger perpetuated by attempted perfectionism is that you may never push yourself enough to learn that it's okay to fail since you are afraid to do so. Then you keep waiting and working to make everything perfect before you present, speak, or try anything, which means you present, speak, and try nothing (since none of us are actually perfect). Then, when you finally do fall short (and you will), you can't stop thinking about what you could have done differently to have avoided it. This can trap you in a destructive loop.

This type of thinking, where you relive situations, constantly assessing where you could have done better, is often referred to as rumination. It's a common tendency for those who suffer from or have tendencies to perfectionism. It is marked by the internalization of mistakes, leading you to blame yourself for anything and everything that went wrong or was not *perfect*.

And do you know what a perfectionist often ends up deciding when this happens? They think, *Oh, if I had just been more perfect, everything would have been okay.* A degree in psychology is not needed to understand how messed up that is.

A *Harvard Business Review* article titled "Perfectionism Is Increasing, and That's Not Good News" outlined some research fielded by the World Health Organization, noting that we have hit a record number of young people worldwide suffering from depression and anxiety disorders.[13] They directly link this finding to a rise in perfectionism, stating that it is an "impossible goal" and that "those that become preoccupied with it inevitably set themselves up for failure and psychological turmoil."

---

13 Thomas Curran and Andrew P. Hill, "Perfectionism Is Increasing, and That's Not Good News," *Harvard Business Review*, January 26, 2018, https://hbr.org/2018/01/perfectionism-is-increasing-and-thats-not-good-news.

Of course, striving to be your best self is a good instinct. It's the part about holding yourself to a standard that, by definition, is impossible to achieve that's kinda insane.

Now, Create *Your* Story: Disempower Perfectionism

Fact: Perfectionists tend to achieve LESS and stress MORE than regular high achievers.[14] So if you are obsessed with perfection or have unhealthy perfectionist tendencies, it may be taking a toll on both you and the people around you, while not getting you any closer to reaching your goals. Being detail oriented is one thing, but if you constantly beat yourself up or ruminate over your mistakes, it can lead to all sorts of issues.

The Merriam-Webster dictionary's definition of *perfect* is "being entirely without fault or defect." I think we all understand from a practical perspective that is not possible; heck, it is not even *human*. Plus, isn't it our differences—yes, even our imperfections—that make us who we are? So why would anyone strive to be *perfect*? Who decides what that is anyway?

To help us understand if our perfectionist tendencies are at an unhealthy level, Verywellmind.com highlights some telltale traits, including the following:[15]

- **All-or-nothing thinking**

    This is the difference between being satisfied with doing a *good* job versus doing a *perfect* job. If you cannot stop or accept anything less than your definition of perfect, this could be a sign of perfectionism.

---

14   Elizabeth Scott, "Perfectionist Traits: Do These Sound Familiar?" Verywell Mind, reviewed February 21, 2020, https://www.verywellmind.com/signs-you-may-be-a-perfectionist-3145233.

15   Scott, "Perfectionist Traits."

- **Being highly critical**

  Perfectionists tend to judge themselves more harshly than they do others and have difficulty "giving themselves a break" when things do not go just right, leading to low self-esteem.

- **Unrealistic standards**

  The standard of "perfect" is unattainable. This goal leads to a feeling of constantly being unable to be successful at anything, which can be demoralizing.

- **Defensiveness**

  Perfectionists find it difficult to respond appropriately to constructive criticism due to the pain they associate with the less-than-perfect performance that is being critiqued.

- **Procrastination**

  The fear of a less-than-perfect outcome sometimes keeps perfectionists from trying at all, which then keeps them from succeeding—paradoxical, but true.

Your assignment for this chapter is to contemplate the downsides of perfectionism—especially how it can negatively impact your mental health and your relationships, while not getting you any closer to your true objectives. We ruminate on mistakes and blame ourselves and get so angry at our own missteps in ways that would be considered irrational if we reacted the same way to someone else. Why do we do that?

Make a list of ten "imperfect" things you have done recently or you believe about yourself. Write them down. Maybe this list includes something like being late for a meeting/appointment/school pickup, messing up on a presentation, or getting inappropriately angry about something. Imagine if someone else that you care about, say your best friend or a close coworker, had done these things and shared them with you. How would you react? That's right. You would probably be supportive and understanding, saying something like, "That's okay. You'll do better next time." That's because you know one misstep does not define your friend, does it?

Shouldn't you at least be as kind to yourself as you are to others? Oh, and NEWS FLASH—one misstep doesn't define you either!

PERFECTIONISM MYTH BUSTERS

1. _____

   ... and that's okay because it does not define me!

2. _____

   ... and that's okay because it does not define me!

3. _____

   ... and that's okay because it does not define me!

4. _____

   ... and that's okay because it does not define me!

5. _____

   ... and that's okay because it does not define me!

6. _____

   ... and that's okay because it does not define me!

7. _____

   ... and that's okay because it does not define me!

8. _____

   ... and that's okay because it does not define me!

9. _____

   ... and that's okay because it does not define me!

10. _____

   ... and that's okay because it does not define me!

But Wait, There's More

Years ago, I was on a tight schedule to attend a dressy affair at someone's home after a business flight. The plan was for me to go directly to the event from the airport where my husband, Russ, would meet me with our toddler. I know many career moms will relate when I share that to be on the safe side, I had carefully laid out a complete outfit for my daughter to wear to the party before I left. All Russ had to do was dress her and show up. When I arrived, I greeted Russ, who proudly gestured toward our child happily running around in her fancy outfit. My expression went blank. I felt my stomach drop and my anger rise. *He had put her dress on backward!* I couldn't believe it! How embarrassing! What would people think? When I told Russ how upsetting this was, he just took a sip of wine, shrugged, and smiled, saying, "Whoever heard of buttons in the back?" and walked away.

I had a choice. I could let stuff like this, that's so small and silly in the big scheme of things, give me high blood pressure and wreck my marriage, or I could just lower the bar a little—and be happy—even though it was not, well, *perfect*.

Over the years my opinion about the concept of perfectionism has sometimes caused confusion. Many seem to believe that we should try to be someone else's definition of *perfect* to be successful in life. However, I think that can be one of the most disempowering beliefs you can have. I am sometimes asked with a bit of surprise, "So what you're saying is that being a perfectionist is a bad thing?"

My response is that if you constantly compare yourself to others and put pressure on yourself to be something that is, by definition, impossible to achieve and then berate yourself when you do not achieve it to the point that it negatively impacts your self-esteem, your life, and the lives of people around you, it is abjectly unhealthy. So yes, it is a *bad thing*.

This is generally followed up by something like "So you're a mom, a wife, and a successful businesswoman. How do *you* do it all?" My short answer is "I don't."

My oven is dirty, my bed often remains unmade, we have weeds in our yard, and our basement is a disaster. My kids don't always eat healthy food and have gone to school without lunch, with the wrong outfit, or with the incorrect school supplies. I've stared blankly at my boss while searching for an answer, have had the wrong numbers in a deck and typos in an important correspondence. I've missed meetings, flights, events, and appointments. My PowerPoint slides have frozen in front of hundreds of people. I've gone to work with baby snot on my blouse, tiny handprints on my skirt, and a dollop of breakfast yogurt in my scarf. I've missed my children's parent/teacher conferences, band concerts, and sporting events.

And yes, I have even missed some birthdays, which was tough, as birthdays were a big deal to me when I was a little girl. I liked to bake and decorate cakes and have themed parties for my kids when they were little, because I wanted my children to remember these important milestones. But sometimes, it was simply unavoidable for me (or Russ) to miss the "big day" due to our travel schedules.

Then I had the realization that, like so many things in life, "perfect" is a relative concept. The key is to know your real definition of perfect in any given situation. In this case, did *perfect* mean being there on their birthday? Or did it really mean creating a great birthday memory? Of course, it was the latter. Instead of getting twisted up in the guilt and "imperfection" of labeling myself a bad mom because I occasionally needed to be traveling on one of my children's birthdays, we decided we would celebrate their birthdays on the day *we said they were.*

The kids did not notice that a lot of their birthdays fell on weekends, but they *did* notice that Momma was always there to help blow out the candles on the theme-decorated cake and give celebratory gifts and kisses. If the goal was to help create a childhood full of treasured experiences, then the goal was accomplished. Looking back, in some sort of imperfectly perfect way, it all worked out—in fact, they probably did not even know about this weekend birthday thing until right now.

> **The key is to know your real definition of *perfect* in any given situation.**

So yeah, if you don't learn to say "and that's okay" when your toddler is running around with her dress on backward at a fancy party and things are not going *perfectly*, you could drive yourself nuts and likely become an unpleasant person. If you have a family and you start pushing your perfectionist standards on your spouse and your children, you will drive them nuts as well, while possibly driving a wedge in your relationships and forgetting the real objective you were going for in the first place.

Einstein said that if you judge a fish by its ability to climb a tree, it will live its life believing it's stupid. That doesn't mean that the fish isn't perfect. It just means the fish is not doing what it was perfectly created to do. Here's the deal—you are already uniquely, wonderfully, perfectly you. You are 100 percent equipped to be who you are meant to be and do what you are meant to do. It will not be a *perfect* process, but the only person who can figure out what that means for you—*is you*. And the best way to do that is to get clarity about the version of *perfect* you are meant to be, and stop trying to be someone else's version of it.

CHAPTER 8

Forge Your Fairy Tale

Dreaming & Doing

> *Vision without action is just a dream.*
> **—NELSON MANDELA**

My Story

My husband and I refer to our life together in two epochs: BC and AC. That is, *Before Children* and *After Children*. For anyone who has kids, you know what I mean. For those who do not have kids, enjoy the ignorant bliss.

We had been contemplating starting a family when we were each offered expatriate European assignments in late 1997 and decided that would be a great "last hurrah" of our BC epoch. An expatriate, commonly known in business as an "ex-pat," is, put simply, when a US citizen is sent by an American company to work in a foreign country for an extended period.

In our case, although both assignments were on the same continent, they were not in the same country. For the coming year,

Russ would be working for his management consulting firm in northern England, and I was going to be working in France for Mattel.

Specifically, Mattel asked me to take a special assignment that had not previously existed. My job was to facilitate the important licensing relationship between Mattel and Disney to help grow the business across the European market. Having already attained the title of director at Mattel, I had high hopes of becoming a vice president at the company when I returned.

This was a near *fairy-tale* assignment. My brand focus had moved from the Barbie Business Unit to the Disney portfolio, which, in fairy-tale form, included the Disney princesses. Paris is arguably one of the quintessential fairy-tale cities. Plus, an opportunity like this was exactly why I had chosen to get an MBA with an emphasis in international business. I clearly had earned the trust of my company, and my investments were paying off with an amazing "wish-come-true" global opportunity!

Of course, it wasn't all exactly like we had imagined, in that my husband was going to be located on the other side of the English Channel. But since Russ had already been working for a management consulting firm, we were used to seeing each other only on the weekends. Besides, he had negotiated a round-trip plane ticket to or from anywhere on the continent for every weekend—so every Friday, either he could fly to meet me in any country in continental Europe, or I could fly to see him in the United Kingdom, enabling a year of amazing travel.

Furthering my fairy-tale assessment of the assignment, when I visited England, we would be staying in a converted castle where his consulting company had placed him, located not too far from the royal Sherwood Forest of Robin Hood fame.

We packed our rented little white stucco house in Hermosa Beach, California, and took everything we owned to Nebraska, where it was stored at the family farm. Next thing you know, we, including my cat (yes, the same one that came to NYC), were on our way to Europe.

This new role had been requested by Disney. So interestingly, I was going to be in the rare circumstance of being a Mattel employee assigned to an office space inside the Disney European headquarters. At the time, these offices were located in an incredibly beautiful facility on the most renowned high fashion street of Paris, right off the Champs-Élysées, known as Avenue Montaigne.

My official title was the director of European marketing for Mattel's Disney Business Unit. At the corporate level, both companies simply felt that there was more collective opportunity for Mattel to sell its Disney-branded toys in the European market than the current business represented. The collective teams in each of the affiliate-country markets had been doing a good job but were underindexing compared to the performance of their US-market counterparts.

By 1997, Disney had enjoyed a renaissance of animated movies that is often noted as starting in 1989 with *The Little Mermaid* followed by a string of hits through the 1990s, including *Beauty and the Beast*, *The Lion King*, *Pocahontas*, *The Hunchback of Notre Dame*, and the planned *Hercules*, slated to premiere during my European assignment. Mattel had the licensing rights to manufacture and market the toys based on these films, in addition to evergreen lines like Mickey Mouse and the popular Disney Princess line.

Disneyland Paris (which features Belle's castle from the France-based *Beauty and the Beast* instead of Cinderella's castle like most of their other parks) had opened a mere five years earlier. Because of the extra exposure, both companies felt the subsequently raised consumer engagement with the Disney brand in the market provided untapped opportunity. They just needed to get the affiliate countries to work more synergistically. Of course, I understood the basic assignment, but I did not get many instructions before heading out on my adventure. My new boss in Los Angeles, who was the head of the entire Disney Business Unit at Mattel, only had two words for me before I boarded the plane for Paris: "Fix it."

When I arrived, I'm pretty sure some singing birds and friendly mice helped me as I happily settled into my flat in the Seventh Arrondissement (a section of Paris) on the Left Bank (which is the south side of the River Seine). It was a classic building with a tiny, rickety elevator and huge, ornate, forest-green French doors (of course) facing a little café that I would frequent. From my fourth-floor vantage point, I could see the Dôme des Invalides from one window and the top of the la tour Eiffel from another. Although, to be fair, my view of the Eiffel Tower required climbing onto my kitchen counter and peering out of a small, oddly shaped pane from an uncomfortable angle. That part is generally removed from my more romanticized Paris stories, even though I have admittedly climbed up on the counter to gaze at the famous lighted landmark on a clear night, perhaps with a nice glass of Bordeaux.

My commute to work turned out to be a daily blissful stroll, over Pont des Invalides, crossing the Seine, past the beautiful storefronts of high fashion brands, to my new job in the City of Lights. Along the way, I would grab a croissant and some coffee, ordering in my best French and saying, "*Bonjour!*" to the passing people—a little like Belle from the opening scene of *Beauty and the Beast*. It was fun to gleefully imagine how the famously aloof Parisians might have been confused by my poorly accented friendliness.

Without a doubt, I was an outsider. An American in Paris. An English speaker on the continent. A Mattel employee in the Disney offices. But by now you know being in an unfamiliar environment was nothing new for me.

On my first day at work, I confidently walked through the ornate gates of the Disney European headquarters and, with calm tenacity, explained to people who spoke English as a second language that I was *supposed* to be here, even though I was not a Disney employee, all while managing to secure an office assignment and get an IT guy to set up my computer. Pretty good, huh? *Oui!*

I was unpacking files from the boxes that had been preshipped, which were *finally* "discovered" in the mailroom after a lot of confusion when a nasty crackling sound permeated my new office. This was followed by a bright spark and some smoke. I immediately turned toward my workstation to see the legs of the IT guy still sticking out from under my desk, as my French vocabulary was quickly expanded to include the word *merde!* (No, I'm not going to translate what he said.) What a way to announce the presence of "the new American"— by trying to catch the building on fire while curse words flew from my office door. So much for day one.

My first week or so was focused on just getting acclimated and meeting some key people in the Disney offices, including the very impressive head of Disney Europe. All of that was great, but there was a job to do. Then, after my many meet-and-greets, there finally came the day when I sat alone in my new office with a cup of strong French coffee only to face an odd and unexpected dilemma. It was one of the most terrifying things a businessperson can see—*a completely empty calendar!*

From my exploratory discussions, it was clear that the senior executives in both companies were well aware that I had an assignment of facilitating the teams across both organizations to create more synergy and increase the European sales. Of course—they had conceived it.

However, it seemed that the teams that I was sent to facilitate did not completely understand "why" nor "what" I was *facilitating*. There was no formal or hierarchical authority to do my job. I did not have an admin to set up meetings. I did not have a team reporting to me. Is it possible to drive results when tasked to get people to take action with no formal authority?

Then, my eyes widened as I thought back on what my US boss had said before I left, realizing that the "it" I had been tasked with "fixing" involved two separate companies and touched scores of individuals located in cities scattered across a number of European countries. Well, it's not like anyone has failed getting the countries of Europe to agree in the past, have they? Okay, you don't have to be a world history major for your stomach to drop at that thought. Oh my! Maybe this was more of a nightmare than a fairy tale.

While taking another sip of my strong French coffee, I let this sink in for a moment. Most large corporations, including Mattel, are structured in organizational layers, with people operating within a defined and calendarized process that includes nearly daily check-ins assessing what to do, who was doing what, and when things were due. The process itself drives action and momentum. All my management training and experience had been in a traditional, hierarchical reporting structure. Now my boss was multiple time zones (and an ocean) away, and I was the boss of, well, no one, and in charge of "facilitating."

How was I going to do this? There were no agreed-to project lists or preliminary discussions on the appropriate strategic approach, no suggestions about how to work with the teams in each country or affiliate office. Just "fix it."

Finishing up my last buttery layer of croissant, I stared straight ahead as the realization hit me that this may be a near-impossible task, requiring a level of persuasion and informal authority that I had never had to muster, in an environment of multiple cultures and languages.

Again, no team. No budget. No relationship with the people in the European offices of either company. My mind was racing as a whiff of the lingering smoke smell from the recent IT accident filled my nostrils while only one word ricocheted through my brain: *merde*.

"Oh, my goodness," I thought, "I'm kind of like a … uh … (gasp) *management consultant!*" Upon my new epiphany, it was clear that the next step was to immediately call that management consultant husband of mine who was up in Derbyshire, England. I needed to talk this one out. I picked up the phone and frantically fought through the international dialing protocol.

"How am I supposed to 'fix it'?" I passionately exclaimed. "I don't have a team or a budget. I don't have *any* formal authority. Hardly anyone even knows who I am!"

Russ listened and then calmly said, "That's right, hardly anyone knows who you are."

Well, that's a pretty terrible way to cheer up someone, I thought. I did not respond. He paused and said it again, this time slowly. "Hardly … anyone … knows … who … you … are."

We were still kinda new to this marriage thing, but seriously, how was that supposed to help? Was he trying to make me feel *worse*? Russ eventually tried again with a different tactic. "What would you do if you felt like you *did* have formal authority, a team, and a budget?" he asked.

Well, I had an answer for that! First, it was important to get clarity on the corporate goals, the financial objectives, and the prioritization of Disney properties. Then it would be critical to meet with both the Disney and Mattel affiliates in the key countries, probably the biggest one first, to listen to their issues and understand their business plans for the year, as well as share the corporate objectives and talk about best practices and challenges. That would help me identify some commonalities, so I could share those best practices from region to region, which didn't seem to be happening as often as it could, based on my initial conversations. Then, I could facilitate better communication between the individual country affiliates and those teams at the corporate leadership level—perhaps even advocate for them—with the goal of improving the overall business results.

"So do that," Russ said.

"What do you mean? Do what?" I asked.

"Sharon, you said it yourself," he continued. "No one knows who you are. But you have been assigned a job. You clearly understand what to do. So just act as if you have the authority to do it. Because you do."

Mais oui! But of course! Why hadn't I thought of that before? The solution had been right under my smoke-filled nose all along.

The objective was to "fix it," and as my long spew of next steps would attest, my concern wasn't *what to do*. The tactical next steps were clear. The concern was grabbing the reins when I was in an unorthodox situation.

I had been assigned—handpicked, in fact—for the role by the head of the Disney Business Unit at Mattel and approved by the head of Disney's European headquarters. The authority was there; it just wasn't so obviously bestowed!

How liberating, I thought, tapping my fingers together, repeating, "Nobody knows who I am! Bwah-ha-ha-ha!" No, just kidding, I didn't do that—but it would have been funny if I did.

(By the way, what happens next is what is commonly called a plot twist in a Disney—or any—movie, where a story starts one way and then turns in a different and unexpected direction.)

Then, instead of sitting around waiting for someone to officially give me a green light to take action toward the goal, I began to *act as if* I had the authority and started *doing* my job—until someone told me not to. That's right, there is one consistent thing that stands between having a dream and achieving a dream—*doing* something about it.

Not a moment was wasted. That afternoon, a plan was detailed that included a financial spreadsheet and a marketing template for each affiliate to complete, along with a calendar that included visiting each affiliate country, starting with the largest, Germany.

The next day, the call was made to the German Mattel affiliate office. I used my high school German for the first time in nearly fifteen years, said, "Guten Tag," and introduced myself as the new director of European marketing for the Disney Business Unit. "I'm

> There is one consistent thing that stands between having a dream and achieving a dream—*doing* something about it.

working out of the Disney European headquarters in Paris," I said, adding, "and I've been assigned to help facilitate and drive the sales of the Mattel/Disney-licensed products. I'll be in Frankfurt in two weeks, and it would be wonderful to meet with your team along with the Disney team. I'll be sending you a template to fill out beforehand, so we can have a robust discussion. Look forward to seeing everyone then!"

Holy *merde*! It worked!

This approach was repeated for other affiliates in countries including Italy and Spain until I had set up the first round of meetings in all the key countries. My travel itinerary and newly created schedules were sent back to my boss at Mattel, *as if* this was exactly what I was supposed to be doing. Which then, by default, *became* exactly what I was supposed to be doing. Everything was approved, and my corporate credit card was reimbursed. Good sign.

As my strategic plan took me from country to country and the meetings progressed, I shared the best ideas from country affiliate to country affiliate. Because of some of the great promotions and translatable marketing concepts that were being implemented, we decided to have a conference at Disneyland Paris, where the Disney and Mattel affiliates could each share their country's success stories *together*, as a way of kicking off the planning cycle for the following quarter and agreeing to a collective go-to-market approach.

In this case, my "acting as if" had to do with stepping up, creating my own momentum, and learning to be a leader without someone in a more important position pointing me in the right direction or pointing at me and saying, "Follow her." By *acting as if* I was a leader, I therefore *became* a leader.

Understanding the dynamic of where formal power and informal power intersect is critical. Without this knowledge, you may misinterpret power. People may follow others for a short time because of bestowed formal power, but loyalty and trust are why people follow others in the long run, and that's where *informal* power comes from. It is earned through the creation of relationships and mutual respect. The best bosses work on the informal power, even when they have the formal power—which usually comes through practicing something known as "servant leadership."

> People may follow others for a short time because of bestowed formal power, but loyalty and trust are why people follow others in the long run, and that's where *informal* power comes from.

In every culture (country or corporate), breaking down barriers, facilitating and opening communications, enabling people to understand objectives, identifying and setting shared goals, supporting and driving toward desired results, and celebrating success is a winning recipe. This is the way humans work. Not Disney, not Mattel, not the French or Americans—*humans*. Bringing the teams together to create comradery and relationships matters. Then, teams want to win together (not so much as individuals, companies, or countries), and over time, exchanging best practices becomes a regular, organic process that perpetuates success.

I thought I had a vision of how to succeed at this ex-pat fairy-tale assignment, but without "acting as if," it would have remained an unattained wish upon a star. By embracing the informal power of the position and enabling the teams to work together, we drove a double-digit revenue increase for the Mattel/Disney business that year across the European affiliates as compared to the prior year.

 # A Question from the Heart

ARE YOU DREAMING BUT NOT DOING?

Does this sound risky to you? Acting "as if" you are, or that you have, something that in actuality you are not, or don't have?

In my case, what I did not have was the *formal power and authority* to achieve the assigned goal in a traditional manner. I was plunged into an ambiguous situation with loose and informal oversight. It would have been easy to just say, "So what do they expect me to do?" Then I realized that I did have an option. I just needed to take the action to make the authority real.

Therein lies the fairy-tale *magic*, such that it is. If you are waiting for somebody to bestow something on you or recognize your potential, instead of living your potential and letting them catch up, you might be waiting a long time. Isn't a promotion really just a formality—a public acknowledgment of something that's already effectively happened? The majority of the time, you have already shown the signs of achieving or deserving the next level. That's why you get promoted, not the other way around.

The real risk is *not* doing anything. Harkening back to *The Power of Positive Thinking*, author Norman Vincent Peale wrote, "The 'as if' principle works. Act as if you were not afraid and you will become courageous, as if you could and you will find that you can."

Everyone from TED Talk speakers to writers for *Psychology Today* have explored this basic idea. It can be simply explained by smiling to make yourself happy, versus believing you need to *be* happy *before* you smile. Sociologist Robert K. Merton coined this basic idea as the "self-fulfilling prophecy" in 1948. It's true in everything from our confidence on the job to the quality of our relationships. That's right, the authors of an article in *Social Psychological and Personality Science*[16] discovered that even the old adage of "dressing for success" is true and can lead to increased confidence and creativity on the job, while a Columbia University study found that "rejection expectations" can cause couples to behave in ways that invariably result in a split.[17]

There is even a technique called "Adlerian therapy," which is designed to help people overcome their self-defeating views. The idea is for adults to remind themselves what it was like when they

---

16   Michael L. Slepian, Simon N. Ferber, Joshua M. Gold, and Abraham M. Rutchick, "The Cognitive Consequences of Formal Clothing," *Social Psychological and Personality Science* 6, no. 6 (August 2015): 661–68, https://doi.org/10.1177/1948550615579462.

17   Geraldine Downey, Antonio L. Freitas, Benjamin Michaelis, and Hala Khouri, "The Self-Fulfilling Prophecy in Close Relationships: Rejection Sensitivity and Rejection by Romantic Partners," *Journal of Personality and Social Psychology* 75, no. 2 (1998): 545–60, https://citeseerx.ist.psu.edu/viewdoc/download?doi=10.1.1.373.2815&rep=rep1&type=pdf.

played make-believe as children (maybe like Disney princesses). Why? Because acting *as if* you're already the person you want to become isn't just a fairy tale, Dr. Adlerian argued. "As people begin to act differently and to feel differently, they *become* different," he wrote.

Okay, I love a good Disney movie as much as anybody, but simply wishing upon a star probably won't get you there. It seems the secret magic in the fairy dust is activated when you confidently combine actions aligned with your goal along with feeling as if you have already achieved it.

Now, Create *Your* Story: Act As If

Nelson Mandela said, "Vision without action is just a dream." The vision is necessary to have something to model. Stated simply, when you decide to "act as if," you must also ask yourself, "As if *what?*"

You have your Goal Tree. You have written your One Hundred Wishes list. You have fired your negative committee. You are not stifled by perfectionism. It is time to embrace who you are **becoming** and **act as if** it is already who you **are**.

In this exercise, describe who you are becoming by *visioning* it. It is five years from now: Where do you live? What kind of clothes are you wearing? What kind of car do you drive? What is your fitness level? What kind of social life do you have? What is your job? Who are your friends?

Then "act as if" all of that is already true, just like the Adlerian theory suggests. Really, it can be empowering and fun to try this—even if it is just in small ways—and see what happens.

"ACT AS IF ..." WHAT?

I WILL ACT AS IF I WERE A PERSON WHO ...

- lives in a home like _____
_____
_____
_____

- has a partner who _____
_____
_____
_____

- works at a company that _____
_____
_____
_____

- drives a car like _____
_____
_____
_____

... add your own and now embrace your new self!

- _____
_____
_____
_____

- _____
_____
_____
_____

- _____
_____
_____
_____

But Wait, There's More

Toward the end of my yearlong assignment in Paris, the team at the Disney European headquarters was happy enough with the results they decided to host a celebration dinner, bringing the Mattel and Disney affiliate partners from each country together to toast our accomplishments. It was one of the most extraordinary gatherings I've ever attended. We were invited to Disneyland Paris after hours to take a special trip on the infamous *Pirates of the Caribbean* ride. Somewhere in the middle of the well-known water excursion, the boats abruptly stopped, and we disembarked to have dinner right in the middle of an animatronic pirate scene. We dined and laughed and toasted our wonderful year and our new relationships. Dressed in formal attire, Mickey and Minnie even stopped by to say hello.

Shortly after returning to California, I achieved my objective by earning the title of Vice President of International for the Disney Business Unit at Mattel, which would now require me to coordinate strategies and facilitate communications for all the affiliate countries around the globe—not just Europe.

Indeed, my year in Europe had been a fairy-tale adventure, but not the way I thought it was going to be. I had not been magically or publicly bestowed with the pomp and circumstance of royalty or formal authority to do the job like a princess would have been. On the contrary, despite not having been crowned, it was my decision to knowingly "act as if" I already had the authority to do the job, to embody it, that made the difference that led to success. (Frankly, as a tom*girl*, I *never* understood why Rapunzel didn't just cut her own hair and use it as a rope to climb down from the tower by herself!)

Maybe I was not a princess at all. Maybe I was more like a pirate of the Caribbean. Not in a murderous, pillaging kind of way, but in the willingness to operate with an unorthodox approach, when required, and the savvy understanding that real power, true leadership, and influence actually exist far beyond their formal attribution.

Just when I thought my fairy-tale adventure had come to its "happily ever after" culminating with my promotion, we discovered that while in Europe, yet another magical thing had happened: Russ and I were now on the verge of welcoming our AC epoch with a little princess of our own.

CHAPTER 9

A New Dawn

Failure & Flying

Forget about the consequences of failure. Failure is only a temporary change in direction to set you straight for your next success.
—DENIS WAITLEY

My Story

Ten days early, on the Sunday after Thanksgiving in 1998, our first child entered the world. But that was not going to be the only big change in store for me and Russ.

We were about to learn that one of the hardest parts of being married is finding a balance and respect for each other's dreams. We were also going to get a little taste of what it means when you stand in front of a preacher and say, "for better or worse."

An opportunity for Russ to leave his big global firm and join a smaller consulting company was in the making. It would be a great move for him, but it was headquartered in Chicago.

After five years of evolving my career at Mattel and achieving my VP goal, I was looking forward to going back to my job after maternity leave. I did not want to leave my company, my friends, or the sunshine of Southern California.

After some difficult conversations (that surely included me having my hands on my hips, or maybe one hand on my hip and an infant on the other), we finally reached an agreement and made the decision to move to the Midwest where Russ had more connections (having attended school in the Windy City) and where we would be closer to his Nebraska roots (and the newly minted grandparents).

Although this was a logical move and being closer to family is a reasonable and common next step for young couples with new babies, most everyone who knew me was shocked at this change, including my boss at Mattel. Frankly, it was even shocking to me as I listened to the well-rehearsed resignation come out of my mouth in his office. It was clear that I did not know if I wanted to, or if I even could, embrace this new unfamiliar role of stay-at-home mom. But I had decided I was willing to take this opportunity to try it on for size. (Frankly, although I could not have told you this at the time, I know now that so many of my moments of growth or insight have come from this type of *uncomfortable* decision.)

Admittedly, I'm from a generation where many of our mothers found great pride and satisfaction in raising a family and running the household, which is a beautiful thing. However, my grandmother was a teacher, and although my mom took time off while my brother and I were little, she worked much of her adult life. Plus, I was inspired by the numerous female role models from years past who had chosen a different path, which helped to pave the way for future business-women, despite that the culture at large often still encouraged them to accept a more traditional path.

My new goal: adjust to a new baby, in a new city, in a new house, and kinda with a new husband—as most of our relationship at that point had been in different cities, countries, or time zones due to his work and travel schedule. That's all.

I joined a mommy group. I strolled a bundled baby over the icy suburban sidewalks of the Chicago winter. I made a few friends with women in the neighborhood. I worked on turning our 1930s bungalow into a home. And I thought, *Look at me—I'm doing this!*

With the last remnants of the piled-high snow finally melting, Russ returned from a business trip to find another over-the-top home-improvement project completed (this time I had refinished the stairs). While I was completing dinner and putting the baby in her high chair, he blurted out, "You need to go back to work."

Ignoring some wood stain from the stairs still on my arm as I stirred the vegetables, I asked, "Why? I'm fine!"

"Because you're going to drive both of us crazy." As you've probably noticed, Russ has a tendency for blunt honesty. But it wasn't as bad as it sounded. He knew I loved spending time with our firstborn, watching her grow and learn, but he could also see there was a desire for more external stimuli. Plus, I think he was a little worried that I might try to build on a playroom or something.

I could not deny that I felt a little out of place in the mommy group at times and had trouble connecting as the conversations drifted away from business or politics toward diaper rash and recipes.

After the timer buzzed and I removed the casserole, Russ lifted me up onto the kitchen counter, oven mitts still on my hands. He got right in my face. Deep down, part of me thought he was about to explain how I needed to go back to work so I would stop cooking, but it was much bigger than that.

"I want to be crystal clear," he said, firmly but lovingly. "If you're staying home because you think it's something I want you to do, you are wrong. If the roles were reversed and we moved to Chicago because *you* had a job offer, I know you wouldn't expect the same of me. You wouldn't want me staying home and climbing the walls. Why would you think I expect that of you?" Russ was right—all of this home-improvement effort was a cry for help, and he knew it.

He continued, saying that he would support me if I really did want to stay home. "But I think you've got to do your thing." He paused and added, "I know who I married."

Really? Well, maybe I didn't know who he married. I loved my daughter, but I loved having a career too. I liked being at home, but I really enjoyed engaging in business-centric topics and challenges including strategic problem solving and leading teams. It was confusing.

Although the discussion with Russ took some of the pressure off, it was an entirely different interaction that stopped me in my tracks and provided the final clarity needed. One of my neighbors just happened to be a psychologist (yes, really), and she walked into my life at that exact time (again, yes, really).

We were having an early spring picnic on the front lawn with our children. I told her about my conversation with Russ. Like a good friend (and therapist), she knew that the key to helping someone have their own personal aha moment often means asking questions more than making definitive statements. She paused and queried, "Tell me again why you wanted to stop working and stay home in the first place?"

"This is not about me. I want to do the right thing for my daughter," I told her. "I want to make sure I'm being a good mom."

"Okay," she said, as we both paused to instinctively check on our babies—sippy cups full, diapers empty—before returning to the conversation. Then came the mic-drop moment as she nonchalantly asked, "Do you want your daughter to sacrifice her dreams for your granddaughter?"

I had to replay this question in my head a couple of times to really understand it, and then I confidently answered, "Of course not!"

She looked up and caught my eyes, sternly adding, "Then don't model it."

Wow. She was right. She had spoken a truth that I had been afraid to think, let alone say out loud. Being a good parent isn't just about being present for your kids; it's about setting a good example. Maybe if you want them to be empowered, to live up to their full potential, you should attempt to show them what that looks like—by living it the best way you can.

Just realize that if your dream is a career, there is going to be some give and take, especially if there is a spouse and kids in the picture. There will be times when you could have been a better parent, but you were distracted by a presentation with a deadline. And there will be times when you could have done a better job preparing a presentation, but you were distracted because you needed to scrub a brand-new tube of lipstick off of your toddler, who thought it was a great idea for her legs to be colored a lovely shade of "mauve burst."

If your dream is to be a full-time parent, as it is for many women (and a growing number of men), that is a wonderful thing too. So if you are afforded the opportunity to do so, model that! It is not about *which path* you are modeling; it is about teaching our children to be their authentic selves by being your authentic self.

Whatever you choose, just make sure it is your truth and not a compromise that's actually someone else's dream or a preconceived societal norm. I also understand there can be some realities of life and economics that don't allow everyone to live their dreams in this regard. I am hopeful, however, that with a supportive family and improved social structures, more people are able to follow their passion, and if that includes a desire to combine a family and a career, it can more easily coexist. This opportunity, particularly for women, has been hard fought by those who've gone before and is sadly still not even close to possible for many around the globe.

> It is not about *which path* you are modeling; it is about teaching our children to be their authentic selves by being your authentic self.

My friend continued to drive home the point. "If you truly love your daughter and your family, and I know you do, never forget that the very best mom is a happy mom. So contrary to your statement, it *is* about you, at least much more than you think—because what makes you happy makes for a happy family."

Her words had released me. Released me from the imagined guilt, confusion, and potential internal conflict of going back to work. Within a week of this conversation, I received a call from an executive recruiter for a job with a toy company in the greater Chicago area. Kismet?

From that, I enjoyed a rewarding experience as the VP of product development and marketing for the US toy division of VTech, the multibillion-dollar Hong Kong–based company, which in the '90s was mostly known for making real phones and low-tech "not so real" computers and other electronic learning toys for kids.

However, because I had simultaneously been poking around for something entrepreneurial, I stumbled on the fact that one of my favorite childhood toy brandmarks was for sale, so I decided to take a shot and explore the possibility of purchasing it.

First introduced by Topper Toys in 1970, the Dawn line of dolls had been introduced a little over a decade later than the ubiquitous Barbie doll. But they were different in many ways. For one thing, Dawn dolls were almost half the size, just six and a half inches tall. They could fit in the palm of your hand or in your pocket, so they were easier to carry around. Additionally, Dawn dolls had four main characters that were a racially diverse group of friends well before that was the norm.

As a toy executive, I found it odd that boys' action figures had made a transition to a more friendly, handheld size some years ago. Although Hasbro's G.I. Joe had started out as an eleven-and-a-half-inch product in 1964, almost all the human-esque products for boys, commonly called "action figures," had evolved to be on a much smaller scale.

Why? I couldn't help but wonder if a smaller size might be more desirable for girls and possibly a potential competitive advantage. Plus, Dawn dolls' diminutive dimensions should allow the product to be sold at a more affordable price point, which was one of the reasons they outsold their behemoth pink competitor in unit volume in the early 1970s.

It was even more intriguing after learning that Dawn dolls had not been forgotten. Vintage Dawn dolls were turning up on internet auction and resell sites, fetching hundreds of dollars, especially when they were MIB ("mint in box") or NRFB ("never removed from box"), which is a big deal in the toy collector world. There were books, blogs, and websites celebrating these dolls that hadn't been sold in toy stores for decades. Plus, since the doll was introduced in 1970, the year 2000 would mark the thirtieth anniversary of Dawn.

Anniversaries can be great catalysts to remind the public why they first fell in love with a brand. Being at Mattel during Barbie's thirty-fifth anniversary in 1994 taught me that you never want to let a good reason to celebrate go to waste. It provides a tug of nostalgia, an opportunity to revisit something from our youth, and a chance to rediscover the warm, happy feelings it once gave us and can even provide a great reason to introduce a brand to a new generation. Plus, '70s pop art, fashion, music, and style from the Dawn era were back in vogue. Yes, this could be an interesting and fun adventure.

My plan was to first leverage the nostalgia and the latent brand awareness of Dawn to launch a commemorative collection of thirtieth-anniversary dolls in the specialty toy and doll market. If that was successful, we could then introduce a new, more contemporary version of the dolls in the mass market.

This specialty toy store retail segment has all but disappeared now, largely pressured by the superior bulk buying and pricing power of mass merchandisers and, more recently, the shifting consumer shopping habits and the broad selection offered by online stores. But in 1999, there was still a meaningful number of these small toy and doll shops, lovingly referred to as "mom and pop" stores in the United States. Surely some successful public relations exposure, driven by the anniversary and nostalgia positioning, could generate enough sell-through of the collector dolls to serve as a great setup to secure a retail test in the larger channels to launch an updated version of Dawn for today's fashion doll fans?

After Russ agreed with the rationale and the business case, I bought the brand from a well-known toy inventor company and got to work. The launch of something like Dawn requires design, development, packaging, legal, copy, safety, manufacturing, sales, accounting, importing, marketing, and account management. That's a lot of hats.

This was one of those moments when I was surprised at how much I did know but also realized how much I *didn't* know.

In his spare time, given that he was one of those CPA/MBA guys I was talking about earlier, Russ did the heavy lifting on setting up the company as a business entity and creating the processes and systems, as well as setting up the accounting.

We identified a factory in China to help develop the dolls and began working on the tooling (the "mold" for the product), perfecting the face paint and the arm and leg movement and mechanism, selecting the hair, and sourcing the fashions. In the final phases, it was necessary for me to fly to China to sign off on the prototypes. Everything was going fine until the factory could not figure out how to replicate Dawn's signature pleated white miniskirt from the original doll outfit. This was critical to being authentic, which is an important element for the collector market and certainly for any sort of anniversary launch.

Exhausted and jet lagged, I sat in a typical China toy factory meeting room, which can be stark, cold, and bland, while being asked to decide which one of the numerous white fabric swatches to use instead of the petite pleated material that was iconic to Dawn's original skirt, which would undermine my ability to launch the product as a "replica." I did not like any of them. This was a problem. Just then, the factory manager walked through the conference room door to introduce herself.

At Mattel, I had spent weeks at a time in Hong Kong and the China mainland working on Barbie Fashions each year, so the social protocol was quite familiar to me. I rose and greeted her with a slight bow and executed a formal exchange of our business cards. We smiled and shared some hot tea as she asked me how the project was going. I explained the situation about the skirt and handed the tiny vintage fashion with the problem pleated skirt to her to examine. Her eyes widened, and to my surprise she responded, "Wow, I have worked on this product."

"What do you mean?" I asked.

"Well, years ago when I was a factory seamstress, I made this dress," she continued as she examined the little aqua halter frock with the white skirt. She turned it inside out, looking at the construction of the item, and added, "Hmmm, I think I remember that we did not use regular fabric for this skirt. We used a prepleated ribbon." Mystery solved!

Another member of the team ran out of the room to return with multiple large spools of white pleated ribbon. We were able to match the original skirt exactly. Truly unbelievable. Dawn was on her way!

In 2000, with some positive public relations coverage and sales of the thirtieth-anniversary doll, everything looked promising. Russ joined team Dawn and we introduced an e-commece site, rented an office, and hired someone to fulfill both the internet sales and wholesale shipments.

As planned, in early 2001, on the heels of the anniversary collector launch, we secured a regional spring test in Toys 'R' Us for a reimagined, more modern version of Dawn and her friends designed for the current girls' market. When the test results came back positive, we agreed to a national launch of the brand. Then, I called in a few personal favors so we could produce a television commercial to introduce the new Dawn dolls. How exciting! We ordered our products for the following holiday season and awaited the arrival of the container from China to support the chain-wide shelf set at the biggest toy store in the United States, just in time for Christmas.

And then the 9/11 disaster happened.

The terrorist attack of September 2001 was shocking and devastating. Along with every other American, I was horrified and angered. The loss of innocent lives and the feeling that our American ideals were under siege was a terrible moment for our nation and the world. So many people suffered personally because of that day, far more than we did, so in no way am I trying to overstate this circumstance. Nevertheless, we had a situation on our hands.

Each year it is estimated that more than eleven million maritime shipping containers full of almost anything you can imagine arrive at America's seaports.[18] That September, one of those eleven million containers headed to the US shores from China was floating somewhere in the Pacific Ocean filled with our entire Dawn doll holiday order. People had worked for months and made thousands of dolls and sewn tiny fashions with little white pleated skirts and put them in thousands of boxes, all of which were scheduled to dock at the Long Beach Port in just a few weeks—already paid for with a big chunk of my savings and a whole lot of sweat equity.

Then, after the initial shock of the situation, the next call we had feared came. Toys 'R' Us canceled the entire order.

When the boat showed up in October, we incurred even more cost by storing the Dawn dolls in a warehouse while we tried to figure out what to do. My only hope of avoiding a huge loss was finding somebody to purchase them at a discount. We ended up selling them for half price to a mall-based store that has since closed, called KB Toys. Now what?

---

18 US Customs and Border Protection, 2019.

A Question from the Heart

CAN YOU RECOGNIZE WHEN FAILURE MAY BE A FLYING LESSON?

It is nearly impossible to see how failure can be of benefit in the moment it is happening. Steve Jobs, who famously endured being ousted from his own company, Apple, only to rise again, once said, "You cannot connect the dots looking forward; you can only connect them looking backward."

This was an emotional and confusing time for me. Not only was I facing the end of my business venture, but I was also thinking about how I had begrudgingly quit Mattel to move to a city where I knew no one—with a new baby. How I had recently been by my mother's side as she lost her multiyear battle with cancer. And how shortly after that I had a miscarriage. Then, at three months pregnant with our second child, 9/11 happened, which simultaneously upended the psyche of the country and marked the end of my entrepreneurial dream.

To add insult to injury, I had poured myself into relaunching Dawn dolls as a way to emotionally deal with some of those challenging events. Now it was all down the drain.

The strategy, the idea, the marketing, and the product were great. Leading up to the anniversary doll release, the media exposure was nothing but positive. I was interviewed on CNN-FN, had a shout-out in *Elle* magazine, and was featured in many of the toy, doll, and collector magazines. A new collector's book had been published about Dawn dolls, and I was asked to pen the introduction. I sold the thirtieth-anniversary Dawn doll collection on QVC. We even won a "Dr. Toy" award for the new version of the product that had been successfully test marketed at Toys 'R' Us.

Honestly, one of the most difficult parts of dealing with this was realizing that if I had to do it all over again, I would probably follow the same game plan. And yet, it still failed. It would have been easy and understandable for me to have gotten into a downward spiral.

Clearly, I have been sad and confused and not sure how to take the next step forward, and I wanted to share this because I understand no one wants to hear any advice about how to get over failure if you believe the person giving the advice has never endured failure.

After a lot of thought, I decided that the key to overcoming failure is to entirely redefine the concept. When you can do this, you can also redefine your life.

I am not the first to have this personal "revelation," mind you. When Thomas Edison was asked how it felt to fail at making the light bulb one thousand times, he famously responded, "I didn't fail one thousand times. The light bulb was an invention with one thousand steps." The truth is, Edison, as well as any number of well-known inventors, businesspeople, artists, and athletes, had likely mastered some version of this concept to help him "redefine failure," whether he realized it or not.

> The key to overcoming failure is to entirely redefine the concept. When you can do this, you can also redefine your life.

Now, Create *Your* Story: Redefining Failure

The approach I have used to rethink failure requires you to choose between two **wheels**—one puts you on a downward spiral, and the other puts you on an upward spiral.

First, which wheel you get on is determined by how you label the concept of failure itself. For the purposes of this exercise, instead of deciding that failure is abjectly "bad," let's just start by defining "failure" as simply a term that we place on an unexpected outcome or event that seems undesirable in the moment.

Second, you need to understand if you have a natural tendency to *internalize* or *externalize* the reasons for the outcome of the event that has been deemed as negative (a.k.a. "failure"). Not that you don't want to own your mistakes and try to improve, but extreme internalizing can be debilitating, while learning to externalize even some of the reasons for the "failure" can be empowering. Here's how:

THE FAILURE WHEEL

When you completely *internalize* the reasons for the undesired outcome that you have labeled "failure," you then tend to overly blame yourself, which leads to associating the experience with *pain*. Pain leads to fear of trying or taking a chance again because you don't want to fail again, since you are linking that to internalized pain. *Who do I think I am? I can't do this. I already know I'm going to screw it up.* This is how you get on the **Failure Wheel**. Then, the attempt to achieve your goals starts a downward spiral—perhaps to the point of not trying to reach them at all.

THE SUCCESS FLYWHEEL

When you can *externalize*, or at least depersonalize, the reasons for an undesired outcome, you are more likely to see the learning opportunity; then you can be empowered by the situation by looking at it as a source to acquire knowledge. With more knowledge, you end up with more confidence, which increases the odds that you will try again. With the improved approach and more confidence, you are more likely to be successful the next time you try. *That's okay, I'll get it next time. I'm glad I learned this now so I can plan for it later. I can't wait to try again.* This is getting on the **Success Flywheel**. As in, your willingness to learn and try again causes your success and potential to start to fly. Which in this case means, what we commonly refer to as "failure" can become a catalyst for future success.

REDEFINE FAILURE

THE FAILURE WHEEL

REDEFINE FAILURE

THE SUCCESS FLYWHEEL

Hopefully, whatever you are attempting won't take one thousand times like it did for Edison, but (even though I encourage bold goals) most of us probably aren't trying to do something as game changing as inventing incandescent light. Just remember, no matter what your goals, you are significantly improving your odds of success with this approach.

Dawn did not work out like I had planned. Not even close. However, in the spirit of Steve Jobs's quote, there is a direct line that can be drawn from this experience to my subsequent career success. Learning the toy business from the inside out put me in a unique position to elevate quickly at my next company in the industry. And even seven years later, I was told by my new boss in an entirely different industry that my entrepreneurial background (on Dawn) was a key reason he wanted to hire me.

Okay, contrary to the well-known saying, maybe some of my darkest moments were actually right *after* the "Dawn," but I have learned that just because you can't see the sun does not mean it isn't there. As the quote from the beginning of this chapter notes, "Failure is just a temporary change in direction."

But Wait, There's More

A few years later, when the child who was in my tummy on 9/11 was around four years old, I came home to find a very flustered babysitter.

A number of crystals from the light fixture had crashed onto the dining table and shattered because my young son had apparently flung himself off his top bunk, which was located directly above the dining room, landing on his floor with enough force to cause this crazy accident.

He was fine, but still in time-out.

I went directly to his room, which was decorated in honor of his favorite baseball team, to find him sitting on his lower bunk, not looking especially sad, guilty, or fearful. "So what happened?" I asked.

He turned to me, with a little-boy grin and a hint of pride on his face, and said, "I was trying to fly."

I thought for a moment and was quite pleased with my obvious parenting skills when I decided to inquire in a very Dr. Phil manner, "And how did that work out for you?"

Do you know what that kid said? He shrugged and told me enthusiastically, "It worked!" He then paused and added, "For a second!" Wow. That made me smile. Not because it was funny. I was truly delighted by this assessment.

He had hit the ground *hard*. For many, that might be considered an utter and complete failure. But he had immediately translated that event into success because, well, "It worked … for a second."

Think about how beautiful that is. "It worked for a second." In that moment, I was like, *Holy smokes, this kid has discovered the secret to life.*

There's a famous baseball umpire, Bill Klem, who called the game from 1905 to 1941, back before there were video replays. One of his best quotes was "It ain't nothin' till I call it." What he was saying is that no matter what the players, the coaches, or the fans thought the call should be, until he decided and gave the signal for out, safe, or strike—it was "nothing." This is the same concept.

My son was officiating his own game, and he was calling this play a "home run." So that is what it was. And who am I to tell him any different? In his mind, he accomplished his goal. And you know what? Technically, he *was* airborne—for a second.

I encourage all of us to have a crazy dream, to be willing to take some action, maybe even break some crystals, and then, no matter what happens, have the infectious spirit of a kid amazed about how he actually just *flew.*

Fail or fly? It's up to you. Cuz it ain't nothin' till you call it.

CHAPTER 10

Time to Transform

Challenge & Change

> *The only constant in life is change.*
> **—HERACLITUS**

My Story

Now what? Did *both* Russ and I want to go back into the corporate world, or just one of us? Were we staying in Chicago, or moving the family again? No matter how you saw it, after Dawn, we had some decisions to make.

We had two small children now, and neither one of us wanted Russ to go back on the management consulting road. He liked the multidimensional, quick-study aspect of the job but did not want the crazy travel anymore. The tipping point was when our toddler daughter wasn't quite sure who he was one Friday evening after his return flight for the week. He just couldn't keep doing it.

Interestingly, the Dawn experience had revived Russ's entrepreneurial penchant, while it reminded me how much I enjoyed and thrived in a larger corporate environment.

We agreed that at least one of us should have a more flexible schedule so we could maintain the involvement we desired in the lives of our growing family. After a multiday discussion (and maybe a spreadsheet or two), my husband, who some might refer to as a "guy's guy," suggested that the most strategically sound decision with the highest potential was for us to support *my* corporate career, while he explored another, more flexible, entrepreneurial opportunity. I did not see that coming.

My first networking call was to my previous boss at Mattel—you know, the one who told me to "fix it" when I went to Paris? He was now an executive at Disney Consumer Products, the division that licenses the Disney brands to other companies so we can enjoy things ranging from beach towels to coffee mugs featuring an image of Mickey or Cinderella. After a day of meetings in Los Angeles, I thanked him and shared how intrigued I was about the opportunity but noted I was a bit concerned that Russ may not want to move back to California.

Without missing a beat, he reached for the phone and asked, "Does Russ like New England?"

"Yes, why ... and, uh, what are you doing?" I responded.

He was calling Brian Goldner, the head of the US Toy Division of Hasbro, the huge New England–based toy company. My previous boss told Brian that I was the perfect fit for what he was "doing over there." (What could that mean?) In short order I was on my way to the other coast to interview in Pawtucket, Rhode Island, the location of Hasbro's headquarters.

Hasbro and Mattel were, and still are, two of the largest toy companies in the world. They both began as family-run businesses, but they have different sensibilities and personalities. In a nutshell, Hasbro is an East Coast organization mostly known for G.I. Joe and superheroes, while Mattel is a West Coast company mostly known for Barbie. Hasbro's headquarters are in a refurbished factory near the Seekonk River, while Mattel's are in a high-rise with executive offices offering a distant view of the Pacific Ocean. One is green camo, and the other is hot pink. Yes, Hasbro was different from my first major toy company employer. But that was okay. I was different too.

Since my first day at Mattel a little over seven years before, I had gotten married, lived in Paris, had my first child, moved to Chicago, worked at VTech Toys, started my own company, endured some life-changing personal losses, had my second child, and experienced the end of my entrepreneurial endeavor in conjunction with one of the most devastating events in US history.

In 2002, despite some recent acquisitions and a "vault" of well-known brands, Hasbro had been through a tough time, even enduring layoffs in 2000. However, unlike Mattel, which had comparatively fewer brand assets to exploit, Hasbro oversaw a vast treasure trove of household names in the toy and game industry, including Monopoly, My Little Pony, Mr. Potato Head, Playskool, Transformers, Littlest Pet Shop, and Nerf, along with some of the most powerful licenses in the business, like Star Wars. Unfortunately, the value of this brand power was not showing up in the company's overall performance or stock price.

My early meetings at Hasbro included a lovely lunch with Alan Hassenfeld (the then CEO and grandson of one of the founding brothers who started the company in 1923, naming it "Hasbro" for the *Has*senfeld *Bro*thers). I also met with Brian, who outlined his vision of what he believed Hasbro could become if the company could stop thinking and acting like a "toy company" and start thinking and acting like a "house of brands." Over the years, these well-known brands had built consumer resonance beyond toys, and he believed that Hasbro just needed to access the value of these brands in a more meaningful way. He wanted to throw open the windows and get some fresh thoughts inside the company. And he wanted people who could be a part of executing that vision. *So that's what he was "doing over here,"* I thought.

I couldn't help but be reminded of my time on Barbie a few years earlier. By doing just what Brian was talking about, Barbie had become a juggernaut in girls' fashion, entertainment, collectibles, *and* toys. In other words, the Barbie business wasn't just about a *doll* anymore; it had evolved to what is known as a "lifestyle brand." With Hasbro's broad range of toy and game brands, if they wanted to create a playbook to systematically monetize this amazing roster of household names, this could be a really exciting ride. Brian ended that meeting with one of my favorite sayings from him: "There are no tired brands, only tired marketers." Now *that's* a challenge I still take seriously.

By the end of the New England trip, I had secured a position as the VP of Tiger Toys, a small division of Hasbro that consisted of the remnants of a company that had been acquired in 1998. Tiger was best known for creating a cultural phenomenon and one of the best-selling toys of all time: Furby, the small animatronic creature that spoke its own Furbish language.

I dug into my first assignment on the Tiger business soon after moving our young family to Rhode Island. In addition to running the existing product lines like HitClips, I was asked to oversee the launch of two new concepts: one called VideoNow, which was brought to Hasbro by a bold outside inventor, and the other a mechanical lifelike cat that had been developed by a brilliant internal engineer. It didn't take long for me to determine that there wasn't a lot of heart for either of these projects from the internal sales force. In fact, when I introduced myself to Hasbro's head of sales as the new VP of Tiger, he responded without looking up, "What's that?"

Oh my. Maybe this was not such a great idea after all.

But with my recent personal hurdles and newfound determination to turn that entrepreneurial "failure" into a "flywheel" for success, a fire had been lit in me. Russ and I had agreed to let my career take center stage, so I needed to make this work. I was in my late thirties, and in some ways, it felt like I was starting over. I felt like this was my last chance to have a meaningful career breakthrough after the recent Dawn setback following all of that early success. Okay, maybe I wanted to prove something to that sales guy, but more importantly, I wanted to prove something to myself. No tired marketers here!

Even though the Tiger team only had a few new concepts to work with for the next holiday season, I found that small, talented, and driven group ready to cook with gas. I put a handmade sign in my office window that faced the internal main corridor. It read, "THE KITCHEN" with a subtext of "Don't come in if you can't take the heat!"

VideoNow was a small, proprietary disc player that was designed for kids to watch their favorite cartoons and shows on the go. Getting this concept to the finish line was going to be an uphill battle, even though it was still a few years before portable DVD players or screens in cars were widely affordable. It had a tiny black-and-white screen (Would kids watch that in a world of color TV?) and a fifty-dollar retail price point (Would parents pay that in the *toy* aisle?).

Somehow, we had to make this product a holiday "must-have." They had already landed on a pretty sleek logo and handheld design.

Our goal was to quickly secure the best possible content and devise a comprehensive marketing strategy that would be supported by a killer ad campaign aided by a hook line that had already been dreamed up by a former Tiger executive.

We were down to the wire trying to close a deal for top-notch content, knowing, no matter how cool the video player was or how impactful we made the commercial, if there was nothing good to watch, it was doomed. Finally, the call came, and I flew directly to NYC during a family vacation on Cape Cod for a last-minute meeting to secure a deal with Nickelodeon, which included the ever-popular *SpongeBob SquarePants* library—just in time for the launch.

The puzzle pieces were falling into place, but we still had a big problem. It was getting late in the selling season, and our largest customer was not on board with VideoNow because a key buyer did not believe in its potential. This was a serious issue. Without this account buying the product, the entire business model would fall apart.

This retail corporation's divisional buyers were coming to Hasbro to finalize selections for the following Christmas season. Fourth quarter is when toy companies make or break the entire year, so this was a pressure cooker presentation with the future of the item (and my opportunity to make an early impact at Hasbro) on the line.

> The puzzle pieces were falling into place, but we still had a big problem.

The team pulled research on kids' viewing habits, the importance of children having a closed entertainment platform with only "kid-friendly" content, and the value of keeping kids happy and quiet during long road trips. I polished the presentation late into the night while sitting at my kitchen island, taking a brief break to give good night kisses to a pair of kids in footie-pajamas as Russ marched them upstairs for story time and bed. The pitch hinged on VideoNow being a holy grail of toys by meeting core needs of both constituents: kids *and* parents.

The presentation theater at Hasbro is called "The Tank." There are a lot of legendary stories from those who have presented from the pit of this sunken half-circle theater. For me, this was one of them. The lights dimmed as my presentation popped up on the big screen behind me. I was on. I shared the research and included some funny personal "mom" insights supporting the data. We finished with a music-driven, highly energetic commercial rough cut that we had recently completed, featuring a bunch of cool kids pushing the product forward in a disruptive MTV-esque way, with an end scene of them all yelling, "I want my VideoNow!"

When the lights came up, everyone was smiling. Everyone, that is, except the buyer who had not wanted to carry the product. The consensus had changed. Not only were they interested in VideoNow for the holiday season—they wanted to put "try me" displays at top-tier stores and create their own commercial for the product! It was beyond what any of us could have hoped for. VideoNow went on to become one of the big Hasbro hits of the season.

As for the mechanical cat—which the sales guys had given the loser nickname "The Fur Brick"—it was another surprise hit and ended up being the catalyst for launching the successful FurReal Friends brand, which has had a long and prosperous run for the company.

Plus, the head of sales became an ally and great counsel. Not bad for my first year or so.

With that little bit of earned respect from two relatively unex-pected holiday successes, I felt emboldened to ask if there might be a better way to position the Nerf brand. (I had great memories of my brother teaching me how to throw with the iconic foam football from the 1970s.) Recent attempts to (re)popularize the brand for a new generation had fallen mostly flat. The sales had declined to a small percentage of its height. And around 2003, with the goal of reinventing the brand, it had been given an image overhaul with a new "edgy" logo that looked like it had been spray-painted on an abandoned building. It just didn't seem like it was going in the right direction to me.

With the support of my boss, Hasbro created a new division by combining Tiger and the sports/action brands of Nerf and Super Soaker designed to combat the shrinking tween business (defined as kids ten to twelve years old—that is, in be*tween* being a young child and a teenager), which was being squeezed by the growing impact of video games and a phenomenon that had been coined as KGOY (kids getting older younger).

On Nerf, we first shifted the personality and logo of the brand back to something more sports oriented. Then, we focused on the blaster and dart business. One, because there was already a low-priced knockoff brand in the "regular" foam football category that had origi-nally made Nerf famous, and two, we thought the blaster positioning was more like playing a live-action video game (plus, the Hasbro engineers had some really awesome concepts in the pipeline).

While we were still landing on a new ad campaign, I made another Tank presentation to the internal sales team to share our progress on repositioning Nerf. We showed them the new sporty logo and explained our intention to bring back a nostalgic tagline for the relaunch: "It's Nerf or Nothin'!" One of the top sales guys immediately quipped, "Well, I guess it's *nothin',* then." I'm also pretty sure I was hit with a Nerf dart. Tough crowd.

But this Nerf team was driven to overcome some real challenges across a broad range of "you gotta be kidding me" stuff and worked together to create a great new product line supported by another high-energy commercial. The new advertisement was for an innovative Nerf blaster where we decided to include and feature "vision gear," so we could show the kids playing in a more realistic way. This commercial was the beginning of a new trajectory for the brand. The Nerf business was built over the next few years to become multiple times its size, far eclipsing its all-time sales, and has now become a consistent top-selling brand for the company.

Shortly thereafter, I was awarded with a surprise (off-cycle) promotion to senior vice president (SVP) in the last month of my thirty-ninth year. (I like to think my boss pushed it through early partially because I had shared a personal goal with him during one of my previous reviews of becoming a SVP before I turned forty.) With that, it was starting to look like Russ's calculations for us to follow my career might be right.

Other promotions followed, including one while I was still on maternity leave with our third child, and one where I was asked to choose if I wanted the "girls' business" or the "boys' business" added to my current portfolio. However, because of the support Hasbro had given me, I asked to be placed wherever they believed I could create the most value for the company. Based on my Barbie experience, the decision was for me to bring some fresh insights and energy to the historically much smaller Hasbro girls' division.

Given the string of animatronic hits, we immediately transitioned the growing FurReal Friends business to the girls' division to bring in some new thinking and shore up the mainstay anchor brand of the portfolio, My Little Pony. Shortly after, in 2005, a vault brand that was already in the pipeline when I took over the division was launched—the collectable, stylized tiny animals from the early

'90s called Littlest Pet Shop. It took off like a rocket and quickly exploded into a multimillion-dollar menagerie that had to be aggressively chased with a wide variety of new little critters and complicated assortment management.

Also that year, we reintroduced the famous Tiger hit from the past, Furby. And then, probably unconsciously spurred by all the diaper changing in my home after my new baby daughter was born, I became impassioned to stage a relaunch of another vault brand, Baby Alive, based on the once-popular doll from the 1970s that ate, drank, and pooped. (Which, despite the chatter about how no one wanted to play with baby dolls anymore, became yet another successful launch.)

While all of this was going on, the FurReal team had been diligently working behind the scenes on our pièce de résistance: Butterscotch Pony, an animatronic, three-foot-tall, life-size miniature horse. The impetus for the idea came from the same brilliant engineer who had dreamed up the original FurReal Friends cat. He had shared a sketch with me of an animatronic horse and carriage. I was immediately intrigued.

That led to a string of questions. Could we really create a life-size, responsive fuzzy miniature pony? Should we just do the horse and not the carriage? How much would someone pay for something like that? How would we ever package or sell it in a store? Even with these questions, every fiber of me knew this could truly be toy magic—if we could do it!

You need a lot of conviction to shepherd an idea like this through a company. It was a risky endeavor, and the costly development was only one aspect. We had no idea if the early estimate of a $300 retail sticker price for a toy was even viable at a mass merchandiser. Even in the prerecession world, where the average amount that parents were spending on their kids each Christmas was estimated to be at an all-time high, it was still dicey.

During another infamous Tank session, I reluctantly recommended that we would need to ship the animatronic pony without its head intact to reduce the size of the box, or the added packaging and shipping costs would push the price point out of reach for too many consumers. Brian wasn't enthusiastic, as he rightly worried that kids would be traumatized if they saw a "decapitated" horse in the box. After sharing the potential impact of the added shipping costs, he agreed with the plan as long as we enclosed the head in opaque plastic emblazoned with a message for the parents instructing them how to attach it—*before* giving it to a child.

Shortly thereafter, because of the higher stakes, we decided to visit our top customer instead of waiting for their next regularly scheduled Tank presentation at Hasbro. The meeting almost ended in disaster when one of our tech guys accidentally mixed up the wires, confusing the pony sounds for my demonstration with a sound file for a talking teddy bear. Instead of that incident unraveling the meeting, it simply resulted in some laughter and a couple of *Mister Ed* jokes followed by resounding applause. "That is every little girl's dream," we were told, before eventually securing the holiday order. We immediately got to work on an ad campaign that brought every little girl's dream to life in a magical way.

The calculated risk paid off. The advertising achieved its objective. A top customer gave the pony end cap "try me" displays at select locations, and the sales started rolling in. The wife of (then) UK prime minister Tony Blair was photographed hugging Butterscotch, and, among the plethora of positive PR, it was heralded as "The It Toy" for a comprehensive cover story in the *Boston Globe Sunday Magazine*.

On a personal note, my two little girls were practically in heaven that Christmas morning when they, like so many others, experienced a "dream come true" upon discovering a Butterscotch Pony by the tree—with its head intact. (Okay, sometimes it is fun to be the cool mom.)

At the 2007 New York Toy Fair the following February, Butterscotch Pony won two prestigious Toy of the Year Awards. We were on a roll.

By the next holiday season, the December 24, 2007, issue of *Business Week* featured the girls' division in a full-page article centered around the astonishing growth of Littlest Pet Shop, called "Hasbro's Little Cash Cows." It noted that "the company's toys for girls have soared from $60 million to more than $600 million" in the last few years. To highlight Brian's successful strategy of reviving retired brands with the goal of creating lasting franchises, the article noted, "As Sharon John, head of Hasbro's girls' division puts it: 'No more one-hit wonders.'"

In the meantime, my responsibilities had expanded once again to include the company's crown jewels, the boys' division, which brought my financial oversight to around a billion dollars. This business was not as *innate* for me as the girls' brands, but fortunately, the portfolio addition came when my young son was in the crosshairs of his action figure years. During this time, he carried what he referred to as "my guys" everywhere, particularly his Spider-Man guys and his Star Wars guys. I watched how he played. I asked him questions. I played with him. I learned a lot and applied it to my thinking as we started to reimagine some of the opportunities to continue to grow this exciting part of the business.

However, even though this was Hasbro's wheelhouse, little did we know that the boys' business, in fact the entire company, was on the precipice of a massive watershed moment. After multiple years of vision and toil, we were mere months away from the launch of a game-changing feature film based on the successful Hasbro toy brand Transformers—flying robots in disguise. The concept, toys, and cartoons were originally developed in conjunction with a Japanese company, Takara, and had already been around for over two decades, but in mid-2007, the film turned out to be next level. The original *Transformers* movie hit the market with great fanfare and grossed over $700 million in worldwide box office sales that year. This was not a *kids'* movie. This film was targeted toward consumers who had an affinity to the brand from childhood—basically tapping into the preexisting equity that Transformers had created over the years. It was exciting to attend the premiere to both watch the movie and simultaneously experience firsthand the real-time unfolding of the visionary hypothesis that Brian had outlined years before.

Admittedly, my Hasbro journey from VP of a smaller division to SVP/GM and head of the US Toy Division may sound like one of those cleaned-up, straight-line career stories that I cautioned against in the first chapter, but trust me, it was not completely smooth sailing. Like with any big corporation, there were politics, personalities, egos, and issues.

Brian became CEO, and in 2008 I was an internal candidate for the newly identified role of chief marketing officer (CMO) but did not get the position. Around a year later, Hasbro went through a corporate reorganization designed to realign and break the business into brand divisions managed across the globe versus regional or geographical divisions that encompassed all of the brands. With that type of restructuring, the US Toy Division would no longer exist; therefore, there would not be a need for someone to be the *head* of it.

Although consulted as to which of the new global brand divisions I would prefer, I was eventually assigned to be the SVP/GM of the Global Playskool/Preschool Division. On one side, I completely understood the need to evolve the company and agreed that running the brands and divisions from a worldwide perspective was a strategically superior organizational approach for the company at the time. On the other side, it was a confusing set of circumstances, and, from a personal perspective, it felt a little like a limb had snapped off my tree.

As I had already learned, sometimes there is a deeper meaning or a message in things that happen, but sometimes there is not. I did not know in this situation. Either way, I owed it to the company and myself to keep pushing to do the best I could do and be the best I could be. So after some self-reflection, I took a philosophical page from my first boss at Hasbro who used to say, "Go big or go home." I decided to "go big."

To help me stay motivated and focused, each morning when I walked into my beautiful office (the same one Brian had occupied when he shared his vision with me all those years ago as the head of the US Toy Division), I smacked a whiteboard where I had scrawled a huge "AA." It was my secret shorthand for "attitude adjustment."

I got to work. I reviewed the research and sales data, which informed a new strategy for the preschool business and Playskool brand. I reorganized and energized my new team and brought in a great first sergeant from one of our international affiliates. It was time to completely rethink this business, which had been conceived by two schoolteachers back in 1928, with a fresh global perspective.

We put together a mission with an internal rally cry to "Bring the 'OO' back to Playskool." We ordered a bunch of big red "easy buttons" that said "OO" when you whacked them for Tank presentations to help us get a sales team, who preferred blasters and action figures, engaged in baby development insights and items like Lullaby Gloworm. We reimagined the product line, and I traveled to a top retailer to secure the brand's position and stave off the waning shelf-space threat before the next selling season.

By the end of that year, we had stabilized the global preschool division; delivered a new, well-received brand look and marketing campaign for Playskool; enjoyed record-breaking sales for Play-Doh; and negotiated a long-term deal for a coveted iconic preschool license, which had been wrangled from a top competitor. In other words, we brought the "*OO*" back to Playskool.

But something was different.

 A Question from the Heart

CAN YOU RECOGNIZE WHEN CHALLENGE IS SIGNALING A TIME FOR CHANGE?

Hasbro occasionally invited its leadership team to weeklong training events at Dartmouth College. That summer's event featured Marshall Goldsmith, executive coach and author of *What Got You Here Won't Get You There*. It's a remarkable book highlighting the need for leaders to develop more self-awareness and a willingness to evolve their management tactics and styles, which often requires jettisoning behaviors that may have proven successful in the past. The title of the book really sums it up. Whatever you have been doing to achieve your current level may be the exact same thing that is keeping you from moving to the next level.

That's right, throughout our careers and lives, we develop skills and habits that serve us well and lead us toward our goals. Until they don't.

I was delighted to sit down with Mr. Goldsmith for a private lunch after his speech to explore how I could improve as a manager and a leader. In our conversation, he reiterated that personal or executive evolution doesn't always mean *adding* new skills. It often means letting go of skills that once felt like invaluable tools. It can be difficult to accept and often hard to do. So hard, in fact, that many fail in the attempt.

To be clear, some of your previously acquired "skills" or tactics that have been instrumental for you to achieve your current level may now be the same "skills" that are keeping you from moving forward. These "skills" have become "bad" habits that you need to break.

As the *Harvard Business Review* noted, "The capacity for reinvention is the single most important career attribute for executives today. Successful reinvention may look different for each of us, but if we do not attempt it, we are sure to fail."[19] If that's too academic for you, how about this quote from legendary UCLA basketball coach John Wooden: "Failure isn't fatal, but failure to change might be."

Unfortunately, the things that need to change or stop are often hiding in a place called your *blind spot*. And the things that are hiding there have stifled untold careers.

Was there something in my blind spot?

Now, Create *Your* Story: What's in Your Blind Spot?

If you've ever played with a Transformer or been a parent who had to figure out how to manipulate one from a vehicle to a robot for your kid, you know that it no longer needs the wheels when it is in flying robot mode. In like manner, as your career evolves, what you may need to operate or succeed while rolling on the ground, metaphorically speaking, aren't the same things that you'll need when you are soaring in the sky.

The stuff hiding in your blind spot can include skills, tactics, actions, or beliefs that need to be changed or discontinued for you to

---

19   Gary Hamel, "The Why, What, and How of Management Innovation," *Harvard Business Review*, February 2006, https://hbr.org/2006/02/the-why-what-and-how-of-management-innovation.

evolve or grow. We *all* have them. If you think you don't, that's probably something in your blind spot. They are there, just like that car traveling behind you in your passing lane that you can't see in your mirrors.

Identifying what is in your personal blind spot, however, is harder than taking a quick peek over your shoulder on the interstate—especially if you think the skill, tactic, action, or belief that you need to change, or stop, has been critical to your success thus far.

Because of this difficult dichotomy, you aren't likely to find these issues without a lot of introspection. But if you have been bouncing off guardrails or having fender benders in your career, this process could help unlock the reasons why. With that, the following provides some recommendations for identifying what could be lurking in your blind spot:

> As your career evolves, what you may need to operate or succeed while rolling on the ground, metaphorically speaking, aren't the same things that you'll need when you are soaring in the sky.

1. Take a look at your personal yearly reviews or corporate assessments from the past. Are there some things that keep showing up in the "opportunities" section that you are ignoring, are convinced are untrue, or have decided are irrelevant? Is there anything that you instinctually answer with a "Yeah, but ..."? These are clues to something that is hiding in your blind spot.

2. Schedule informal chats with your boss, direct reports, and peers. Ask them what you could do to improve and how you can help them. Tell them you want honest feedback because

you want to evolve as a leader, a manager, and/or a teammate. When they respond with a potentially uncomfortable truth, just say thank you and get to work on it. If all they have to say is how "awesome" you are, guess what? You could have something in your blind spot, and it may have something to do with not creating an environment of honest feedback.

3. If you have an opportunity to participate in a professional 360-degree review, do so. A 360-degree review is when people who work under, over, and beside you (thus the name) give you structured but anonymous feedback. It can be tremendously informative, but only if you keep an open mind. You will hear about your strengths and weaknesses. The key is to use it as a learning experience. If you feel the need to challenge or defend certain results, that's a hint about what's in your blind spot.

Of course, you can cruise along in your career without addressing these *blind spot* issues, and you may continue to advance. But just like the guy on the highway who never checks behind him before changing lanes, you could eventually crash. This exercise can be hard, but stick with it. If this were easy, the executive coaching market wouldn't be nearly as big or lucrative as it is.

In the meantime, let's start with some of the things that are commonly hiding in the blind spots of businesspeople and leaders. The following worksheet notes the **Top Ten Blind Spots**, according to a newsletter prepared by Harvard Business School highlighting a survey conducted by The ExCo Group (formerly Merryck & Company) and the Barrett Values Centre.[20] Your job is to honestly self-reflect on this list of well-known personal challenges. You could

---

20   Joan Shafer, Adam Bryant, and David Reimer, "Revealing Leaders' Blind Spots," *Strategy+Business*, April 29, 2020, https://www.strategy-business.com/article/Revealing-leaders-blind-spots.

also enlist a little help from a close but honest coworker or friend. Just doing this exercise could increase your awareness of potential issues, which is one of the first best steps to tackling any problem.

PERSONAL BLIND SPOT REFLECTIONS

PERSONAL BLIND SPOT REFLECTIONS
(WHAT'S IN YOUR MIRROR?)

1. Lack of emotional intelligence?

   Self-observations: _____
   _____
   _____

2. Poor communication skills?

   Self-observations: _____
   _____
   _____

3. Bad at delegation and trust?

   Self-observations: _____
   _____
   _____

4. Poor listening skills?

   Self-observations: _____
   _____
   _____

5. Does not provide visibility and access to team?

   Self-observations: _____
   _____
   _____

6. Challenged time management?

   Self-observations: _____
   _____
   _____

7. Does not share vision/strategy/priorities?

Self-observations: _____

_____

_____

8. Lack of executive presence?

Self-observations: _____

_____

_____

9. Inability to develop team?

Self-observations: _____

_____

_____

10. Not good at conflict resolution?

Self-observations: _____

_____

_____

Note: Even if you are not on a career track, it's likely you still have things lurking in your blind spot that could be holding you back or negatively impacting your life and relationships. There may not be as many professional tools to find them, but you could start with an open conversation with people you trust. One hint that has been helpful for me is to be aware when something—a comment or an action—makes me immediately angry. This is often referred to as a "trigger." Learn to pause and ask yourself, "Why was that upsetting?" There is usually something hiding there that you could work on.

But Wait, There's More

After my lunch with Mr. Goldsmith, I worked to identify some things that could be in my blind spot. One thing that struck me was an inclination to overclarify a point for fear it was not heard or under-stood in a meeting, which could have been a holdover from when I first started at the company. Remember, the head of sales didn't even know that my job existed, so in the beginning this belief may not have been totally unfounded.

My underdog attitude was no longer required given my years of service and positive track record. However, when you feel like you have had to fight so long for a seat at the table, how do you just stop fighting? It can be even harder if you've risen through the ranks quickly and have had less time to adjust (or for people to adjust to you) at each new level. But that's what I needed to do. What was I fighting for anyway?

With that, I consciously worked toward becoming a calmer and more assured leader. I didn't need to *prove* anything anymore. I discontinued use of some of my *go-to* tools of being the antagonist, maybe even the antiestablishment driver, to get results or force traction or a conclusion. I had become "the establishment." I needed to replace that tendency with something known as "quiet leadership," where you are often the last to speak, and when you do, you are asking more questions than making comments or giving specific directions.

Months following this personal insight, and not too long after we had pushed the *"OO"* button on the prior year, Hasbro asked me to participate in a 360-degree review process with a select group of top executives as a C-level succession planning exercise. As part of the process, we were provided with an opportunity to meet with a professional executive coach to review our results.

My coach kicked off the discussion by asking about my career goals. I shared that I thought I could make a good CMO someday. He pushed away from the table and flipped open a folder in a way that concerned me at first. "Well, that's interesting," he said as he perused my results, paused, and added, "Do you realize you could be a *CEO* right now?"

I must have made a "Seriously?" face, as he then leaned in, adding, "Yeah, you scored at or above sitting CEOs on almost every metric. Are you not aware of that?"

Some say that our entire body regenerates every seven years, as old cells die and new ones replace them. True or not, it is inarguable that we can be changing, and not noticing how much. Over the previous seven years, I had evolved through the pressure, experience, opportunities, and challenges afforded by this dynamic Fortune 500 company. Yet it took an unforeseen redirection followed by some introspection for me to stop thinking about where I *should* be going and contemplate where I *could* be going.

My time at Hasbro was a raucous ride that included incredible successes, intense competition, and some difficult moments. The organization had grown significantly during my time there, and it was an honor to have been a part of it. On top of being able to contribute to the creation of significant value for the company and its shareholders, I caught a pass from NFL Hall of Famer Peyton Manning, attended Hilary Duff's twenty-first birthday party, went on the *Ellen Show*, visited Britney Spears on a music video set, met Miley Cyrus at her concert, and rewrote the song "Whip It" by changing the lyrics to "Brush It" as a part of launching a toothbrush called Tooth Tunes, which sold over ten million units—which only represents a small sliver of the absolutely ridiculous "no way" things that make me nearly impossible to beat at the game Two Truths and a Lie.

But perhaps the most important thing I might have done for myself was choosing to look *inside* at what could be lurking in my blind spot following a corporate reorganization and subsequent reassignment. Maybe my thought that "something was different" after that successful year on the global Playskool/Preschool business was right—but that "something" was *me*. I had started at Hasbro with the dogged determination to restart my career as a midlevel executive following a difficult failure and had *transformed* into a seasoned C-level candidate.

As the executive consultant closed the 360-degree assessment folder, I could almost hear the unmistakable clicks, clangs, and whirrs made famous in the film indicating that a Transformer was starting to change. I no longer needed my "wheels" because I did not need to stay on the ground anymore. I had become someone with "wings," if I simply chose to use them.

CHAPTER EPILOGUE

In October of 2021, Brian Goldner, the president and CEO of Hasbro, lost his heartbreaking and untimely battle with cancer to the shock of the entire toy industry and beyond. As such, I feel it's important to emphasize that so much of what happened in this chapter, and what comes next, is linked to what I learned during my time at Hasbro, largely due to Brian's vision, influence, and personal counsel. The day that I resigned from the company, we had a bittersweet heart-to-heart discussion in his office, which ended with him reminding me that he believed that I was capable of achieving anything I wanted to accomplish in life. I have thought back on that moment many times over the years, especially when I needed a boost of confidence, and most recently, in the weeks following his passing. Brian's encouragement, as well as the multitude of memories we shared ranging from hilarious moments to tough-but-fair conversations, will always be with me and a part of who I have become. Thanks BG.

CHAPTER 11

If the Shoe Fits

Grit & Growth

Without continual growth and progress, such words as improvement, achievement, and success have no meaning.
—BENJAMIN FRANKLIN

My Story

Although the Hasbro consultant from the assessment firm had shared something that I didn't know about myself, he didn't know that my first interview in seven years was scheduled for later that day. That's right, almost unbelievably—only a few hours after the completion of that positive 360-degree review that challenged the limits of the goals and possibilities that I had previously established for my career—I was driving to Boston to have a discussion about becoming president of the Stride Rite Children's Group.

When the recruiter had first called weeks earlier, I was uncertain about the opportunity. I didn't think I was quite ready to leave Hasbro, the footwear industry was out of my toy comfort zone, and I was concerned that a divisional president was a stretch for me.

On my way there, I recalled the Stride Rite recruiter discussing the position as a leadership growth opportunity. The division was in need of a turnaround, and she had described the president position as a "mini-CEO" because most of the functional areas reported directly to the role, including sales, retail operations, design, development, and marketing, although there would be some shared services such as sourcing, HR, legal, and IT. This was very different from Hasbro's matrixed structure, which had actually amplified in the reorganization. My mind was racing. Were the results of the 360-degree review right? Was I ready to be a (mini) CEO, right now?

As I pulled into the parking lot, I was mentally noting some intersections of this opportunity with my experience, including mom and kid marketing, consumer-facing branding, and a turnaround track record for brands and business units that I could highlight. Would it be possible to have one foot in some things I knew, like children's marketing and China sourcing, while taking a calculated step into some things that I did not know, like running retail stores and footwear?

Although my interview skills were rusty given a seven-year hiatus, after a battery of meetings and written assessments, I eventually received an offer for the position. Because I was somewhat caught off guard, not yet embracing the idea of leaving Hasbro, I turned it down.

Shortly after, while I was visiting my hometown, the executive recruiter called me again. This time, she got personal and serious. She thought perhaps I did not understand what a good move this could be. She asked me questions about what I wanted in my career. She shared that she sincerely believed if I could successfully turn around this business, I had a strong chance of being recruited to a full-fledged CEO position in about three years or so.

Could she possibly be correct? Indeed, for whatever set of reasons, this particular role had already proven to be a stepping stone for a couple of female CEOs, including Meg Whitman. In fact, she had been the head of Stride Rite before joining Hasbro as the general manager of Playskool. After that, in 1998, she became the CEO of eBay during its early years. That made me think.

Collective Brands, which housed the multibillion-dollar Payless shoe company out of Topeka, Kansas, acquired the Stride Rite Corporation in 2007 and was run by a driven CEO, Matt Rubel. When I told the recruiter that my lack of direct retail experience was a concern for me, she countered that Matt disagreed.

She shared that Matt was known in the fashion and footwear industry as a tough customer—a man with vision who knows what he wants—and in this case, his vision was that he needed someone like me, a branding expert with mom and kid experience, not a "retailer," per se. Basically, if Matt believed I was the one for the job, then I was the one for the job. The recruiter strongly advised me to make a counteroffer.

Ironically, because she called while I was visiting my dad, I ended up negotiating the basics of my new employment package to become the divisional president of an iconic brand while sitting on the living room floor of my childhood home—in the same spot where I had consumed countless bowls of Froot Loops while watching hours of *Mister Rogers' Neighborhood*. That's right, I was taking my next career step not too far from where I had taken my first steps—probably while donning a pair of Stride Rites.

The Stride Rite Company was founded in 1919. Over its ninety-plus-year history, it had expanded beyond children's shoes to include multiple historic footwear brands like Sperry Top-Sider, Keds, and Saucony. The division I would be leading was the Stride

Rite Children's Group (SRCG). We were responsible for the design, development, and marketing of children's shoes under the Stride Rite banner, as well as the other premium brands at the company. We sold them through the three-hundred-plus corporately operated (mostly mall-based) stores to independent shoe stores and large department stores.

After accepting the position, I had dinner with Matt. I decided I would casually, almost jokingly, ask why he wanted to hire someone like me, someone who had no footwear or vertical retail experience.

It was a tense moment. To him this was neither casual nor funny. He put down his fork, looked straight at me, and said that was *exactly why* he had recruited me. He had specifically requested that the head-hunter identify candidates who were outstanding brand builders, who understood the marketing dynamics between young kids and their moms. I was identified as a high potential target because I was running the Playskool business and he thought that my background was perfect. Not my *Hasbro* experience, my *Playskool* experience. Yep, that job I didn't really want. Whoa.

He also said that the world was changing. Retail needed to be completely rethought, and it would be reinvented by people with strategic insights and fresh thinking—people like me. He continued by saying that people stuck in old beliefs would not be a part of the solution. He did *not* want someone with preconceived ideas about how retail of the future should operate. In short, his opinion was that my lack of direct experience running retail stores was positive, not negative. And he expected me to step up and get the job done in short order.

Okay. It was time to put on a larger pair of shoes, maybe even some CEO shoes, if I could find them. It's as true with feet as with people—when you bind them, growth will discontinue. Limit your exposure to new, more challenging environments, and stagnation will follow. Right then and there, I knew if I could stick with this, ready or not, I was about to evolve again, and I needed to embrace it. Matt was going to be a tough, but great, teacher.

Before the official start date, I arranged to meet my new organization in the atrium of the suburban Boston headquarters. Although Matt clearly believed that bringing in someone without footwear or retail experience was a solid game plan, I would soon find out that it seemed no one else on the Stride Rite team shared his belief or enthusiasm.

> Limit your exposure to new, more challenging environments, and stagnation will follow.

Upon entering, I noticed some skeptical expressions. The division had been on a downward trend, and it appeared that none of the team members were convinced some outsider, who knew nothing about the shoe biz, could save it. They stared at me, many with arms crossed. What's this *toy* person gonna say?

It did not help that the New England footwear business has a centuries-long history. More than a few well-known shoe companies hail from the area, and lots of those people know each other. Many take pride in having dedicated their career to the footwear industry, earning the unofficial title of "shoe dog." I had not. I was not one of them.

My speech began with some general background, but it wasn't getting anywhere. Some leaned back in their chairs, stretched out their legs, and crossed them at the ankles. My instincts were telling me to take a different direction, but nothing else was prepared. I paused as they looked at me in uncomfortable silence, only broken by a metal chair leg occasionally squeaking across the hardwood floor.

Then, I asked, "What do you do?" No response. "What do you *do* here?" I repeated with a little more gusto.

Finally, someone blurted out, "We make shoes."

I responded, "Is that *all*? Because I believe you do so much more than that."

I shifted tone and shared a treasured memory from my childhood. When I was little, my grandmother noticed my left foot turned in when I walked. The podiatrist recommended that Stride Rites would help straighten it out, so going to the shoe store with my dad to pick out my new Stride Rite shoes became a ritual. He told me they were special shoes, so instead of feeling like something was wrong with me or my foot, I thought I was really something.

In fact, I had just received a package from my nearly eighty-year-old father that included a pair of my classic white sturdy Stride Rite baby shoes, along with a framed photo of me wearing a similar pair while dressed in a pleated sailor outfit—with my hands on my hips, of course.

After being informed that his little girl was going to work for the company that helped her learn to walk straight, he had climbed into the attic space of my childhood home to crawl around and dig through boxes to find these shoes that he had saved all these years.

I paused and looked at the individuals in the crowd. "You know, we keep our shoes from special events, like weddings or dance recitals. We cherish the memory of our favorite shoes from childhood, especially the ones that we were convinced helped us run faster or climb higher or walk straighter. There's a unique relationship we have with shoes that's a little inexplicable. Maybe it has to do with our very humanity. Maybe it is even linked to our evolution, from the moment we rose and walked."

The demeanor started to shift. Arms slowly uncrossed. Some people leaned in. "So what do you *do* here, really?" I asked again slowly. "You don't just manufacture and sell children's shoes. You create products that help kids run and climb. You help children make special moments that can last a lifetime. You are play enablers and memory makers!"

They say you never get a second chance to make a first impression. This was not the speech I had planned, but it was the speech I needed to give. It was important to connect on a personal and authentic level. They did not want to hear about my career or Hasbro. We needed some common ground that was mission driven.

When I started a week or so later, I knew that Matt, to whom I would be reporting directly on certain aspects of the business, and my boss in the Boston office would expect a new strategic plan in short order, so I started gathering data. I scheduled meetings with key people across the organization, set up calls with our franchise store owners and retail partners, read historical decks, reviewed research, studied financial documents, and counseled with the other divisional presidents. I found many on the team were passionate and driven and ready to evolve, but some were clinging to the past, like Matt had warned. A picture of the situation and a potential fresh direction started to emerge.

Before the entire vision was completely formed and ready to share, I was flying back to Boston from Topeka on a private jet with Matt, and he didn't waste any time asking for an update. "So what's your strategy?"

Not having an answer was not an answer, at least not for Matt. Plus, there was nowhere to hide on this small jet. I pulled out a piece of paper to try to explain what had been forming in my mind—thus far. I sketched out a graph, with the age of the kid as the x-axis and the influence of parents as the y-axis. As the age of the kid increases, the influence that the mom has on their decision-making goes down. I explained how the lines cross when a kid is around five or six years old. That, I said, was the point when the marketing focus should shift from mom-centric to kid-centric, because kids start to make their own decisions, have more brand awareness, and are influenced by peer groups since they have started school or kindergarten.

"And if we've done a good job in the early years, developing a trusted relationship with the mom, the advertising frequency to the kid should decrease because the mom already has a positive propensity to the brand," I continued. "The 'nag factor' should be lower, and therefore it becomes less expensive from a marketing perspective to generate the next sale and drive the lifetime value of the consumer." Perhaps the "holy grail" of toys that I had learned at Hasbro—kid love and mom trust—was also the "holy grail" of children's shoes? He asked some insightful questions and challenged some of my thinking but immediately understood the basic construct, which was my green light to take the initial direction to the next level.

While solidifying the strategy, we simultaneously needed to shore up the fundamentals. I knew this would require a lot of difficult decisions, including letting some people go. There was no way around it. This was going to be a hard slog that would require a lot of grit. This is the tough side of bigger leadership shoes.

Next, even though money tends to hide in similar places when businesses are struggling, it still requires a combination of tenacity, insight, and instinct to ferret it out and attack the causal factors. While you may know where to poke on a spreadsheet, which questions to ask, and what reports to run, no matter how fast you find the issues, you soon learn that getting people to change behavior is the real challenge.

Over the years I have simplified a process to help with this, called "SDSS x 2." Simply put, it's a two-pronged turnaround philosophy: (1) Stop Doing Stupid Stuff, and then (2) Start Doing Smart Stuff. In that order.

It sounds like a joke, I know. But you might be surprised how much "stupid stuff" becomes ingrained in companies. This is not purposeful. People across all levels don't always understand why they're doing things, nor what value those things might be creating—or destroying. Often these things were initiated with a noble cause, but even when the environment has changed or the business needs have evolved, the processes sometimes do not. Nevertheless, this stuff just keeps getting done because it has become routine.

However, in a turnaround situation, if everyone is busy doing things that aren't creating value (stupid stuff), how can they start doing things that are creating value (smart stuff)? As a leader you will hear that they don't have the time. They don't have the mindshare. This is where leaders often make the mistake of hiring even *more* people into an already unprofitable situation to try to do the new smart stuff while allowing others to continue to do the old stupid stuff.

Importantly, none of this is meant to be a commentary on the *people* who are doing the *stuff*. This is about the stuff itself, which only exists because you, as a leader (or someone like you), asked that it be done. By the way, if you are thinking there is nothing happening in your company that is blindly automatic with no benefit, you may need to take another look.

To bring attention to some of the repetitive activities that I thought were outdated, misguided, or generally not creating value, we set aside an entire day for people to ask themselves, "Why do I do this?" The idea was to make it fun and report to the rest of the organization what had been discovered, with no judgment. We called it "Groundhog Day," in honor of the Bill Murray film of the same name where his character kept reliving one day until he got it *right*.

One of my favorite discoveries was a rather large daily report that was automatically sent to one of our printers from another division, which was no longer being used. Each morning, an associate sitting close to the printer simply threw away the report and refilled the paper tray. Groundhog Day caused the associate to pause, locate the source of the report (in Kansas), and request that it no longer be sent. It is so simple but so indicative.

You may think that keeping someone from throwing away a ream or so of paper each day is not going to save a company, but you would be missing that the real lesson is about thinking differently or, better yet, just *thinking*. By the way, it's hard to successfully change the big things, like executing a new strategy, unless you are willing to change the little things, like getting an employee to decide to find out the reason an unwanted report is coming, and stopping it, instead of just tossing out an unused report every morning.

Once we had identified necessary changes and started to streamline the processes, we needed to put new leadership in place and work toward evangelizing the new strategy that had been scribbled out for Matt at thirty thousand feet. Naturally, given the brand, we broke it down into baby steps:

Step 1: Play to our brand history and strengths to parents with children in the "first walker"/toddler space by focusing on our competitive advantage and independent research, which showed that our footwear designs reduced the number of stumbles and falls in early walkers. Create a program to educate caregivers in the importance of proper footwear for children, highlighting that being an *expert* in kids' shoes mattered—good shoes for kids are not simply smaller versions of an adult shoe.

Step 2: Infuse innovation to attract the older kid who had a greater influence on the purchase of shoes with new licenses and "toyetic" products like the "Dark Side/Light Side Star Wars Sneakers" that blinked different lightsaber colors when the child walked.

Step 3: Challenge the brick-and-mortar first, e-commerce as an option, business model that still prevailed at the time (a lot of traditional retailers still considered their own e-commerce as competition). The website address was added to *all* marketing, packaging, and signage. The bonus structure for employees was aligned with the new goals. A new website was launched, and the brand's first loyalty program was designed to fully integrate the consumer and drive lifetime value, regardless of which channel they shopped.

In the end, Matt was right. While he pushed and challenged me on the business side, expecting a new level of leadership and excellence, many of my skills and experiences were transferrable. Specialty retail did need to be rethought, and my lack of "history" was helpful when imagining, assessing, and identifying different possibilities and potential solutions.

It required both grit and growth, but in a relatively short amount of time, the division reversed the negative trend and delivered the most profitable year in its recent history, expanded the revenue of the wholesale business by double digits, successfully relaunched e-commerce, and secured over one million new loyalty members within the first year of introducing the new program. With that momentum, we recaptured our number one share position in the infant and toddler footwear segment, achieved a 12 percent increase in comparable store retail sales, and extended the brand into five countries with new franchise partnerships. To top it off, in 2012, Stride Rite Children's Group was peer-elected as the "Company of the Year" by *Earnshaw's* magazine, which has been considered the voice of the children's fashion and juvenile product industry for nearly a century.

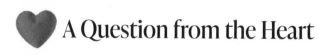 A Question from the Heart

DO YOU HAVE ENOUGH GRIT TO DISCOVER AND ACHIEVE YOUR TRUE GROWTH POTENTIAL?

Years before taking the helm at SRCG, I was shopping with my six-year-old daughter for her new school sneakers, as she had recently outgrown the old pair. She had narrowed the selection to two choices but wanted to try them both again before making the final decision. Sporting the first pair, she ran to the mirror in the store and jumped into the air like an Olympian. Then, she put on the second pair and jumped up and down in front of the mirror again.

She turned to me with confidence and said, "Yep, that was higher!" Spinning around to the salesperson, with her long blond hair swinging behind her, she added, "I'll take this pair." Cute, for sure, but it is more meaningful than that. Those shoes weren't that different. It was simply that she believed one pair enabled her to jump higher than the other—so she did.

In like manner, there was nothing fundamentally different about me the moment I was informed I could be a CEO "right now" by the executive coach during my 360-degree review at Hasbro. I was not instantly sprinkled with CEO glitter and imbued with experience and skills that, up until that point, I did not have. I just needed to believe that I had those skills before I could look in the mirror and see myself jumping to a higher level.

Not only can it sometimes be difficult for you to recognize how much you have grown; it can also be difficult for a company or others in your life to see that you have grown. In fact, others may be *accidentally* anchoring you to your past or the skill, maturity, or leadership level you may have had years before. When that happens, it could be time to consider finding a new environment where you can continue to evolve. Yes, you may need to find a new pair of shoes—a pair that fits better—with a little more growing room.

How much have you grown, and not noticed? How much have you grown, and the people around you not noticed? Considering a larger pair of shoes, so to speak, may lead you to explore a new position or personal environment, which can take a lot of grit. But without that, it's possible that you'll never find out how high you could jump, because you never tried on the right pair of shoes.

Now, Create *Your* Story: Take the Small Steps

Even if you decide it is time to make a big change, like getting out of a constrictive environment, it is important to understand that the little things *you* choose to do and think *every day* have a major impact on your life as well.

While we perpetuate significant personal growth by setting big goals and getting bigger shoes, this is an exercise in recognizing that the *small steps* matter. Although grit is often associated with the larger, harder goals in life, a lot of grit is required in the relentless persistence and practice of making the best small choices daily, which, in turn, can also lead to a lot of growth.

There is a wide variety of data on this subject, but most agree that we have thousands, if not tens of thousands, of thoughts and actions each day, the majority of which are exactly the same habitual

> It's possible that you'll never find out how high you could jump, because you never tried on the right pair of shoes.

thoughts and actions as the day before. These thoughts and actions are the "small steps" in your life. Without taking control of them, you will be accidentally living an individual version of *Groundhog Day*, every day, but *unconsciously*.

With that in mind, it can be fun and insightful to go through your own personal Groundhog Day process. Throughout a typical twenty-four-hour period, ask yourself at every juncture if this is something you should be doing or thinking. Is there a better way to do this? Is this action or thought getting you closer to achieving your goals or becoming the person you want to be?

Your daily journey will no doubt be filled with some "stupid stuff" and some "smart stuff" that you are doing. The key is to identify the "stuff" you are doing and, well, you know what to do next. In that order.

One of the most obvious examples of how the small-step philosophy works is with a fitness goal. To achieve and maintain a certain fitness level or weight takes daily dedication, exercise, and healthy eating. This type of objective cannot be accomplished in one giant step. It takes consistent baby steps—every day.

Lao Tzu famously wrote, "A journey of one thousand miles begins with a single step." This Chinese philosophy is as true today as it was in the sixth century BCE, including the fact that *you* have to take that first step—and every other small step after it.

Review your Goal Tree and determine some small steps that you could take each day that prepare you for and move you closer to bigger achievements. Each one should end with the words "every day." Some examples might be to achieve a specific walking goal—"every day"—or to tell someone special that you love them—"every day"—or to do ten minutes of yoga—"every day."

You've probably heard the trope *Life is a journey, not a destination.* Well, success is a lifestyle—not a moment.

TAKE THE SMALL STEPS

THIS IS AN EXERCISE IN WEEKLY OR DAILY GOALS. THERE
ARE LOTS OF WAYS TO DO THIS, AND I ENCOURAGE YOU
TO FIND WHAT WORKS FOR YOU. HERE'S WHAT I DO:

BUSINESS	HOME
• Example: Attend board meeting	• Example: Call the plumber
•	•
•	•
•	•
•	
ME*	**FAMILY**
• Example: Write in my journal	• Example: Kid's soccer game
•	•
•	•
•	•
•	•

*I like to think about my ME goals as M.E. goals, to remind
myself to always start each day with *M* for meditation and *E* for
exercise. I try to do both each day, but in a wide variety of ways.
Meditation could be as simple as taking five minutes to get in a
state of gratefulness before the day starts, and exercise could
mean a long walk, yoga, or thirty minutes on the elliptical. The
consistency is the key.

But Wait, There's More

Just as I thought I was growing into my new, bigger "CEO shoes" after nearly three years of grit, building a new team, and successfully turning around the division, Collective Brands went through what is known in business as a strategic alternatives process, where a wide array of potential options are explored in order to return more value to shareholders, ranging from a revised capital plan to a transaction to sell the company. This particular process resulted in the Payless shoe division being purchased by private equity and our Boston-based division being sold to a large footwear company called Wolverine Worldwide, headquartered in Michigan.

Before I knew it, Matt, from whom I had learned so much, and my class-act direct boss were no longer with the company. We had an entirely new executive leadership team and an entirely new corporate culture. Our immediate focus became integrating the companies while identifying what is often referred to as the "synergies and redundancies" in the newly formed entity.

I couldn't help but pause and contemplate what my next steps should be. However, before I had time to think about it too much, I received a fateful call. Daddy was in the hospital, having just endured a serious heart attack. He was in a coma and on life support. I had to fly home immediately.

I felt helpless after the doctor left me alone in my father's hospital room, following a briefing about his high potential for brain damage. I sat by his side in eerie silence only interrupted by the intermittent beeps of the machinery that was keeping him alive.

Taking his large hand in mine, I noticed how time- and work-worn it was, yet it still looked strong and solid, like he had been for most of his life. Tears started to flow. They say that your entire life flashes before your eyes when you are about to die. But as I held his once powerful hand in mine, I saw flashbacks of my life *with him*. His sparkling blue eyes smiling at me with pride. Riding high on the shoulders of his six-foot-four frame, where I thought I could see forever. Catching lightning bugs in the summertime. Sitting on his lap as he told his stories. Learning to drive a stick shift sitting next to him in his old green truck. And picking out new shoes at the shop on the town square with him kneeling to mash my big toe with his thumb to make sure I had enough room to grow.

Later that night, when I arrived at my childhood home, his well-read Bible was in his chair, right where he must have placed it the last time he left the house. It was opened to the famous passage in the book of Matthew known as the "Sermon on the Mount."

Moved and still emotional, I read the words from this well-known scripture out loud to myself: "Ask and it will be given, seek and you shall find, knock and the door will be opened unto you. For everyone who asks, receives."

The next day the doctor told me it was time to let him go. It was difficult to get centered. I then did one of the hardest things I have done in my life. I had to allow Daddy to join my mom and brother somewhere else in this friendly universe on a Sunday afternoon in early June. He was buried with them among multiple generations of family, in the shadow of a massive, ages-old hemlock tree.

Over the next few days, I was reminded how much he had struggled with the loss of my grandmother during the summer I conquered that impossible tree—but now from his perspective.

Like Dad, in the aftermath of the passing of my last living parent, I needed to sell my childhood home in a matter of months. In the weeks that followed, I prepared the house for the market. It took days of alternating bursts of energy followed by sporadic crying, triggered by the most random things: a card, a drawing, a toy, a scent, a photo. Even so, I cleaned, packed, or discarded truckloads of memories and objects from my youth, which included finally giving away my mother's clothes, throwing out the bulletin board of dead flowers and newspaper clippings that my parents had kept on the wall of my bedroom all these years, and tossing my now melted Barbie camper, pom-poms, old stuffed animals, and even more Stride Rite shoes from boxes tucked in the crevices of the attic.

The entire time, the words *Ask and it will be given, seek and you shall find. For everyone who asks, receives* kept repeating in my mind.

One can't help but contemplate life in the wake of the death of someone close to them. While still in my fortieth decade, I had buried my last direct family connection to the place I grew up, so a lot was running through my mind. My children were growing up, the company I worked for had been sold, and we had been in New England for about ten years. Was it time for a change? In a moment of hope and exasperation, I answered the repeating biblical demand: "Well, okay, since I'm asking, maybe I'll ask for a fresh start. Maybe a CEO position at a consumer-facing power brand that combines my sourcing knowledge, toy industry expertise, marketing skills, licensing experience, and newly acquired understanding of vertical specialty retail and e-commerce would do. Oh, and why don't we make it closer to Russ's family farm. And how about somewhere I can find a good biscuit or maybe some BBQ?"

What were the odds that a company like that even existed? A million to one, right? But I had already learned that all you need is "possible."

A few months later, not long after the final gavel sounded at the auction of my childhood home, I received a call from an executive recruiter.

CHAPTER 12

Get Your *Bear*ings Straight

Direction & Drive

Life's like a road that you travel on ...
—TOM COCHRANE

My Story

I'm sure you have heard the phrase, *Be careful what you wish for.*

That recruiter call was an opportunity for me to take the helm of a beloved company from the legendary force of nature and founder of Build-A-Bear Workshop, Maxine Clark. Indeed, one week short of a year after the day my father died, I became the president and CEO of Build-A-Bear. And even though I knew in my heart this was the opportunity I had been preparing for my entire career, I also understood it would not be an easy road.

Fortunately, sharing the news at home *was* an easy road. My family was pretty excited about the move to St. Louis. I had been most worried about my eldest daughter, who was on the verge of high school. But oddly, she seemed the most eager. And then, before we took our Midwest house-hunting and school-visit trip, Russ decided to share, "You know, St. Louis has great Southern BBQ, and it is almost *exactly* equidistance between your hometown and the farm! Isn't that something?"

Yes, yes, it is, I thought. Almost like an answered prayer.

We picked up the family and got the kids settled in our new hometown and their new schools, but I had work to do. The company had been experiencing a prolonged period of financial challenges. However, if I was truly in the change-agent business, this was the chance of a lifetime. Despite the struggles from a profitability perspective, the brand power was undeniable. Build-A-Bear was Stride Rite on steroids with good cash flow, a clean balance sheet, and no debt.

As I assessed the situation, consulted with key team members, and pulled on my past, the road map emerged: (1) quickly return to profitability via cost cutting and margin expansion initiatives, (2) identify a long-term strategy that diversified the revenue streams across categories by monetizing what seemed like an amazing amount of untapped brand equity, and (3) despite the company being famously known as an experience-based mall retailer, evolve to be less reliant on the growing concerns around mall consumer traffic while, somehow, more successfully participating in the growing digital economy (without being able to replicate the critical in-store bear-building process online). Executing these three things would take some time and a lot of effort, especially since we would also need to simultaneously (re) build the entire information technology infrastructure, reorganize to support the identified strategy, and most likely bring in quite a bit of new talent to do it all.

That's already a tall order, but I also recognized that the transition of Build-A-Bear, unlike the Stride Rite turnaround, would not have the luxury of being a division of a larger company. Build-A-Bear's publicly traded company status on the New York Stock Exchange (NYSE: BBW) would force us to go through what could be a long and rocky road with the sometimes uncomfortable bright lights of the investor community shining on us at every turn.

I have often said that it seems like Build-A-Bear is the smallest company that *everybody* knows. Being smaller has its challenges, but the statement is intended to speak to what I have always believed to be the strong opportunity for the business. This belief was supported by multiple brand data points, including a 90-plus percent aided brand awareness in North America and impressive affinity scores (that measure emotional connection) that rivaled some of the best-known family brands in the world. I understood this power on a personal level as well, having many special memories of "Pink Stars," the unicorn; "Ruffy," the puppy; and "Springtime," the bunny—three of the many well-loved furry friends that my children had made at Build-A-Bear Workshop over the years.

In the early days of the company, this unique and engaging experience of consumers being able to "make" their own stuffed animals contributed to elevating Build-A-Bear to be a bit of a darling in the specialty mall-based retail space shortly after it launched in late 1997. Following a few years of solid success, the company partook in a highly anticipated initial public offering (IPO) in 2004, which, although successfully executed, unfortunately happened right at the beginning of what has become known as the Great Recession.

The Great Recession (2005–2007) was especially hard on traditional mall-based retail companies. While many retailers (that did not go bankrupt) had recovered by 2012, even after store closures and cost cutting, Build-A-Bear was still struggling with the challenges related to the persistence of the decline in consumer traffic to brick-and-mortar locations, as shopping preferences were shifting to e-commerce. The team was driving hard but not getting as much traction as they needed to reverse the negative trends. It seemed that many understood that the prerecession strategy was not working as planned, but there also seemed to be something else that I could not put my finger on that was keeping the company from rebounding.

It took a longtime Build-A-Bear employee to connect the dots for me. The driving instinct of the organization, she explained, was to keep working to get *back* to their former glory. As such, they were diligently replicating some of the same approaches and using much of the same road map and tactics that delivered success pre-IPO and before the recession. The only problem was that the world had changed. A lot. There was no going back, because what was no longer existed.

But there was something else. As I continued to push on the issue of change, the truth finally emerged. It became increasingly clear that the broader organization was also concerned that if the business model shifted too much, a big part of their corporate culture would be lost. They were afraid that if they changed too much, the company would literally lose its "heart."

Heart has always been a part of Build-A-Bear Workshop, and that was important to Maxine Clark from day one. If you have never been to a Build-A-Bear Workshop, well, first of all, that's just sad. You really don't know what you're missing. In a nutshell, you choose your new furry friend from bins of all types of amazing unstuffed teddy bears, bunnies, and dogs. Then you stuff it, name it, and dress it. But most importantly, at the stuffing station, you also go through the famous "heart ceremony" with a "bear builder" where you make a wish on a small, red "satin" heart and place it inside your newly created plush animal before it is stitched closed. This is a very memorable and special moment that is often emotional for our guests.

Therefore, *heart*—in the small, red, "satin" variety, as well as the metaphorical concept—has always been integral to Build-A-Bear Workshop. Maxine is known to have said that "a hug is understood in every language," and she was at the heart of the culture (as founders often are), so I could absolutely understand how bringing in a "change agent" could be viewed with trepidation, even with Maxine's gracious and vocal support of me.

It was quite the needle to thread. While properly respecting the founder, I had to explain what needed to evolve to effectively address the fiscal challenges while convincing the company that changing, although absolutely necessary, would not "rip the heart out" of the organization.

We got to work on a turnaround strategy to present to the board. Then, following the board's approval, I needed to share the strategy with the corporate organization, or the "Bear Quarters," which is also known as the BQ. This meeting would also include, via phone, district leaders from the stores scattered across the country, the international team from the United Kingdom BQ, and the leadership at the Ohio-based warehouse (a.k.a. the "Bear House"), all of whom were eager to hear the discussion outlining the future of the company.

My plan was to take the following approach to sharing the strategic road map: First, provide some "straight talk" to the organization about the likelihood of the ultimate fatal outcome if we stayed on the current plan and financial path. Second, share the new brand-monetizing three-pronged turnaround strategy to return the company to profitable growth. And third, tell the team that we would make these changes without losing the heart of the company.

As the presentation day drew closer, I became concerned that my plan would not be met with open arms. Buy-in was critical. I needed both minds *and* hearts. A few days before the meeting, it struck me:

maybe I was going about this the wrong way. Although the communication plan was in logical order, maybe it was not the approach needed to encourage and create change in this situation. It was a light bulb moment. I should *start* with the big idea, not the bad news. Be excited about the future first and how our brand, the valuable brand *they* had built, could save the company. Beginning with the ominous warning that we were doomed if we kept operating the same way was a sure way to lose them in the first five minutes!

This presentation was not about strategy; it was about leadership. It was not about business; it was about *psychology.*

The day of the presentation, I strolled through the BQ, which had morphed and expanded over the previous sixteen years from a small space in an office park into a colorful funhouse maze of meeting rooms, workstations, and offices, reflecting the company's growing pains in its early days. It was filled with teddy bears, bright yellow walls, awards, plaques, and framed articles touting Maxine and the company's many successes. Past the oversized bust of Theodore Roosevelt, the US president for whom the first teddy bear was named, was a generous presentation and training room referred to as Bear University, or Bear U. It included a huge drop-down screen and a large stage flanked by two playfully designed eight-foot statues of bear sentinels, standing on spools of thread, with thimbles poised on their heads like helmets—just like the ones at the entrance of the original Build-A-Bear Workshop locations.

> This presentation was not about strategy; it was about leadership. It was not about business; it was about *psychology.*

As planned, I started by getting everyone pumped up about the amazing potential of the extraordinary brand *they* had created.

I shared ideas and opportunities to rethink and expand the revenue streams and monetize the equity of the brand to build the business well beyond mall-based retail or even stuffed animals. I even used a "bear head" diagram to explain the approach.

Then, I shifted my tone and succinctly shared the dire potential future that could happen if the current trends persisted. Choosing to stay the course—and it *is* a choice—would keep this company, *their* company, from ever becoming what it could or should become. The vision I just painted about this beautiful future would be lost.

Once I had their full attention, I added that I believe we owe this to ourselves, our guests, and the company because "Build-A-Bear *matters*! What we do every day *matters*! Providing children now and in the future with a chance to create a special furry friend that they remember for the rest of their lives is *important*! Build-A-Bear deserves to exist!"

People were mostly positive, but the next slide was not what anyone was expecting. It was a larger-than-life photo image of a car's dashboard and windshield. Eyebrows furrowed and confused expressions swept over the crowd. I continued, "There's a reason why a car's windshield is considerably larger than the rearview mirror. It has to do with the comparative amount of time one should be focusing on the past versus looking toward the future."

If we wanted Build-A-Bear to be all it could be, we had to put certain things in the rearview mirror. These things are in the *past*. These things are *behind us*—our previous success, our beloved history and strategies that have gotten us to this point. We are not throwing these things out the window; they will always be a part of who we are, and we can glance back at them for reference, but they cannot dictate our future road. Then I asked, "What happens if you try to drive using only the rearview mirror?"

A few tentative voices piped up. "You crash," they offered.

"That's right," I agreed. "So if we don't start looking and driving forward, which includes assessing the opportunities and choices based on what is in front of us and around us instead of what is behind us, we will crash too."

The analogy continued as people started to lean in. "If you're going to take a long, unfamiliar trip," I added, "you have to create a plan based on your desired destination.

"What is on the horizon needs to be our goals. The coordinates we put into the GPS system are our strategy. What if there's unexpected traffic along the way? We will recalculate our route."

Then I asked, "Who else is in the car with us?"

Answers started coming from the audience.

"Our guests!"

"Our factories!"

"Our licensing partners!"

"Our shareholders!"

"The bear builders in the stores!" The list went on.

The next question was "Who is in the driver's seat?" There was a pause. Maybe they thought I was expecting them to shout out my name, but that wasn't the answer.

"*We are*, together," I reminded them.

"There's a lot at stake," I added. "Basically, here's what we have to decide. Is the world a better place or a worse place with Build-A-Bear in it?"

"Better!" they shouted back at me.

"I believe that, and that's why I'm here."

I explained that the first stop on our journey had to be a return to profitability. Build-A-Bear is a publicly traded company. I asked them if they understood that the board of directors had agreed to award a bonus that year if the company could simply *make one dollar* after the significant loss from the prior year.

"Think about it," I continued. "What if you were a contestant on a game show and hundreds of millions of dollars—which is how much revenue Build-A-Bear generates each year—started dropping from the ceiling?" I started waving my arms in the air, grasping for the imaginary falling currency. "And all you have to do is catch *one dollar* to win!"

I snatched my fantasy dollar out of the sky and held it up to the audience. "One dollar," I repeated. "One dollar out of the millions falling from the sky that we generate. That's all it would take, and you'd get a bonus for the first time in years. Does that seem like a reasonable ask?"

I closed with a reminder that the company needed to change to be successful in the future. The world had already changed, and we needed to catch up with it. "It won't be easy," I told them. "But I believe it'll be worth it. It's your choice if you want to join us on this journey. Don't take this the wrong way, but if you don't want to be in the car—please, no bad feelings—get out of the car. We can't have a lot of backseat drivers complaining about or questioning the journey. We will hit traffic. There will be storms. Roads will be closed. Again, there will be times when we will be doing what the GPS says when we abruptly need to head in a different direction ('recalculating, recalculating …'), but I promise it'll be a ride to remember, and we will drive every mile together, and with heart."

 # A Question from the Heart

HAVE YOU DETERMINED YOUR DESTINATION, AND ARE YOU READY TO DRIVE?

A lot of kids who grow up far from a big city, like me, get behind a wheel rather early in life (tractors, boats, farm trucks), so by the time they turn sixteen and get a license, driving is second nature. Because of that, plus the comparatively fewer things to do in a small town—especially back then—kids spent a lot of time cruising around on back roads listening to music to pass the time. Tennessee is a great place to just drive around. It's filled with beautiful views, rolling hills, and steep ridges, so it is pretty easy to get off course, even when you're familiar with the area. My dad, who knew the county roads very well, was known for claiming to have a "shortcut" to get somewhere and veering onto some gravel or dirt road that would inevitably lead to taking more time than sticking to the original route, which we then jokingly referred to as taking a "longcut."

When taking a "longcut" in the days before GPS, we could just keep driving until we recognized something familiar—maybe a leaning vine-covered barn or some old, rusting farm equipment. All we needed was a landmark, and then we knew which way to turn to get home.

However, no matter how much time you've been driving, what kind of car you have, or who is in the car with you, if you do not know the destination, or you haven't figured out some of the milestones along your journey, it's going to be really hard to navigate how to get there. Knowing your landmarks helps you get your bearings, which is a critical part of getting there—no matter what *home* is for you.

Because of their past success, the Build-A-Bear team had been determinedly driving toward what they believed was the goal. They were making all the *right turns* from the past in the attempt to *get back* to a destination that no longer existed.

This is to say, occasionally, even if you have enjoyed success, there may come a time when efforts are not showing the results that you had seen before, when the landmarks don't look quite right, even when you are doing the exact same things you had been doing. Your desired destination, although previously on the map, may no longer exist or be a viable option. That's your sign to rethink your goal and/ or plan—that is, to "recalculate … recalculate …"

Now, Create *Your* Story: Plan Your Road Trip!

A 2019 article in *Inc.* noted that you can increase your odds of achieving a goal by up to 33 percent if you take these three steps: (1) write your goals, (2) take goal-directed action, and (3) create accountability.[21] The "windshield" analogy I used in the Build-A-Bear BQ presentation provides a fun exercise that covers all three of these suggestions by *Inc.* while pulling together a lot of the discussion points thus far from this book. It can be used to provide clarity for new goals or to "recalculate" goals that are no longer an option or serving your purposes. Are you ready to plan your road trip? Use the following diagram, prompted by the suggestions below, to get started:

- Write down what is in your rearview mirror. What should you relegate to your past? These are things that you want to remember but are no longer useful in guiding your life. They could be things like your childhood memories or where you

---

21   Marla Tabaka, "New Study Says This Simple Step Will Increase the Odds of Achieving Your Goals (Substantially)," *Inc.*, January 28, 2019, https://www.inc.com/marla-tabaka/this-study-found-1-simple-step-to-practically-guarantee-youll-achieve-your-goals-for-real.html.

are from. These are things that you want to glance at to get your bearings, but they are not your destination.

- Write down what you want to put in your windshield. That is your destination. You may want to choose from goals identified on your Goal Tree.

- Write down what you are programming into your GPS. This is your strategy to achieve the goal(s) you put in the windshield. These are the specific turns and tactics (or the little steps) that lead you toward the achievement of your goals.

- Write down who is in your passenger seat. Make sure whoever it is understands the trip they are taking with you and their positive and encouraging role as "copilot"!

- Write down who is in the back seat. Who else is going on this trip with you? Who is critical for you to get to this destination? Who will benefit from you getting to this destination? Is it coworkers? Teammates? Family members? And remember, if anyone from your negative committee is in the back seat, promptly ask them to get *out* of the car.

- Look in the console. There you will find a list of amazing destinations that you will stop at along the way. These are things from your One Hundred Wishes list.

- Check the trunk. If that big stinky bag of limitations is in there, *throw it out!* Is perfectionism in there? *Throw that out too!* Now, write down the things that you are going to need for this trip. These are your values. Keep them safely locked in your trunk.

- Importantly, you must write *your own name* in the driver's seat. That's your accountability.

Finally, you won't get *anywhere* until you turn on the ignition, grab the wheel, put it in gear, and step on the gas. These are your *actions*. This is where you must "throw your (Build-A-Bear tiny red) heart over the bar" and *go*.

Here are some bonus tips for the road:

- Every now and then, take the scenic route.

- Remember to check what's in your blind spot.

- Bring a killer playlist that absolutely must include the origin of this chapter's quote, Tom Cochrane's "Life Is a Highway."

Let's go!

PLAN YOUR ROAD TRIP

YOUR NAME HERE!

What is in your rearview mirror? _____

_____

_____

What is in your windshield? _____

_____

_____

What are you programming into your GPS? _____

_____

_____

Who is in your passenger seat? _____

_____

_____

Who is in the back seat? _____

_____

_____

But Wait, There's More

That "windshield" presentation marked the beginning of the Build-A-Bear turnaround and the internal, corporate-wide "Drive to the Dollar" campaign to achieve the first stated goal of returning the company to profitability. We created "Drive to the Dollar" screensavers. We sent out reminder emails with different ideas as to how to save money, and we gave people permission to question each other's corporate spending, ranging from not ordering pizza for meetings to renegotiating contracts. Some tried-and-true change-management approaches resulted in meaningfully cutting expenses across the organization by reexamining our pricing strategy, value-engineering the product line, and reevaluating the capital spend. However, the team took it upon themselves to also do things such as a supply drive, where everyone turned in their unused office stuff like staples and file folders to be redistributed to other people in the company who needed them.

On that June day, when I made the original kickoff speech, our company was $6 million in the hole. By the end of 2013, we had more than doubled our stock price, and we were able to pay a bonus for the first time in a few years. The collective love for the brand—its promise and place in the world—ultimately was more important and a stronger emotional driver for the team than the fear of change.

However, lasting change management is hard, for organizations and for people. And about six months later, even with our early win, the team had not quite embraced how to *instinctually* think differently, especially in the face of new challenges and continued external pressures.

Having seen this before, in these moments, I like to do something disruptive to remind the organization to stay focused on the change. So in the middle of a quarterly update meeting, we planned for the presentation to be "abruptly interrupted" by a six-foot version of the green clay humanoid from a 1960s children's TV show called *Gumby*.

> The collective love for the brand—its promise and place in the world—ultimately was more important and a stronger emotional driver for the team than the fear of change.

Gumby (well, one of our long-term finance guys dressed in a Gumby outfit) ran from the back of the presentation theater down the middle of the aisle toward the stage, yelling incoherently before leaping onto the stage with me. It was clear that Gumby needed to share something important with us! Now!

A PowerPoint slide popped up, clarifying what Gumby was trying to explain. We needed to do what *he* does to get back on track: First, stay *flexible* in the face of challenge. Second, go for the *stretch* goal. And third, focus on the *green*! People laughed and cheered as I noted that I believed we could deliver on the objectives if we could do these three things. Then I talked a little bit about how real change takes discipline, consistency, and time. To be really (some might say "uncomfortably") disruptive, I then sang Gumby's theme song that I knew from childhood, which ends with "If you have a *heart*, then Gumby's a part of you!"

This admittedly silly but memorable moment shook the team out of the backward slide and ushered in a new internal slogan: "You gotta *bear*lieve."

To this day, we use that mantra, and it remains a part of our corporate culture and language to say that something from the past needs to be put "in the rearview mirror." But most importantly, we had successfully shifted the fundamental culture to be focused on what was in the "windshield"—that is, we were now looking at the road ahead of us, toward our redefined future potential, not at our past.

CHAPTER 13

Beyond *Bear*lief

Trial & Trust

Hold the vision, trust the process.
—UNKNOWN

My Story

"You can't knock the stuffin' outta Build-A-Bear!" is something we sometimes would say, given all that the company had navigated. Just in my years there, we had been through a founder transition, a financial turnaround, and the rebuilding of the IT infrastructure and organization, all while evolving the culture without losing our "heart." In fact, our newly minted mission statement was "We add a little more heart to life."

In the fall of 2015, after returning to and maintaining subsequent years of consistent profitability, the company was invited to ring the closing bell at the NYSE, and I was asked to participate in the pop culture prime-time hit *Undercover Boss*, which became the season-premiere episode in 2016. We were excited to have created what felt like some momentum.

Meanwhile, despite our efforts, the softening macro mall traffic, which had started during the Great Recession, had become even more acute due to continued changing shopper preferences and e-commerce shifts. Some estimates imply that by the end of 2016, the cumulative consumer traffic to malls had *fallen in half* since 2012 (the year before I joined the company). With fewer consumers shopping in malls, we had fewer transactions at our stores and, therefore, softening retail sales.

Adding insult to injury, like a lot of retailers, many of our store leases in these malls were long-term legacy deals that were signed during much better economic times for traditional retail companies. So we were caught in the crosshairs of paying comparatively higher rent with declining consumer traffic for reasons mostly out of our control, resulting in lower retail sales, which was squeezing our margins and, once again, challenging the company's profitability.

As the situation grew more difficult, we (again) quickly focused on pulling a number of levers to cut costs, manage expenses, and expand margins. There simply had not been enough time to begin to capture the planned benefits of the brand expansion strategy. The significant infrastructure and organization investments and changes required to progress our efforts to build new revenue streams and relieve some of the downward pressures on traditional retail were not making up for the declines.

These stressful and changing dynamics were not exclusive to Build-A-Bear. They were played out across a wide array of brick-and-mortar retail companies at such a difficult level that the period has become known as the "Retail Apocalypse," which escorted in a flood of "Going out of Business" signs being posted in and on malls across the nation. In fact, since I had started at the company, reports filled the news highlighting scores of malls and *tens of thousands* of physical store closures along with numerous retailers filing for Chapter 11 bankruptcy protection. Over twenty of these corporate bankruptcies occurred in 2017 alone, according to *Retail Dive*, many of them bearing household names such as Charming Charlie, Aerosols, True Religion, Gymboree, The Limited, Wet Seal, and even a retail chain that had been part of my previous company, Payless.[22] Toys 'R' Us also went out of business that year, taking 735 locations with it, leaving Build-A-Bear as one of the largest independent toy retail chains in the United States still standing.

Meanwhile, on top of some similar "apocalyptic" retail challenges across the Atlantic Ocean, the United Kingdom voted to exit the European Union in mid-2016, which has become commonly called "Brexit." The economic and political aftermath of this vote almost immediately created a material negative financial impact on the company, as about 20 percent of Build-A-Bear's retail business had been historically generated in that market.

It started to seem like every time the company got a little traction, there was another unforeseen negative impact. It was unlike any environment I had ever seen or managed through, and there were times when I wondered if this company, with its new mission to "add a little more heart to life," had enough heart of its own to keep fighting the headwinds. Although we still had all our stuffin', it sure felt like we were taking some body blows!

While all of this was happening, and because of the ongoing uncertainty with both malls and the retail environment overall—plus the subsequent volatility in our stock price partially caused by this market instability—in 2016, the board of directors felt that it would be best for the shareholders if the company initiated an exploration

---

22   Corinne Ruff and Ben Unglesbee, "The Running List of 2017 Retail Apocalypse Victims," *Retail Dive*, December 13, 2017, https://www.retaildive.com/news/retail-bankruptcies-2017/446086/.

of a full range of strategic alternatives. Although the leadership team was enthused about the range of possibilities for the company, and eager and willing to put in the extra time and effort to potentially create value for our shareholders, these processes are often intense and time consuming for executive management. Separately, because of the unknown nature of the outcome at its onset, it is often deemed inappropriate to continue certain investments until there is a conclusion, which can delay future planning and initiatives designed for the company's growth.

> Although we still had all our stuffin', it sure felt like we were taking some body blows!

Over a year later, the strategic alternatives process eventually concluded with a decision by the board to announce a stock buyback program, which is generally considered a "vote of confidence" in the future of the company.

Fortunately, even with some of the strategic investments having been delayed, the team had remained focused on balancing the exploration process and the future, still finding a way to move forward on key projects where appropriate.

We rebuilt our website and launched a new loyalty program, which started to help us drive consistent quarter-on-quarter double-digit growth online.

We redefined our retail paradigm and footprint, creating multiple new concepts and business models for a variety of nonmall locations focused much more on tourist destinations (like Carnival Cruise Lines and Great Wolf Lodge) and multiunit partnership opportunities (like shop-in-shops at select Walmart stores, the largest retailer in the world).

We pushed the envelope as to *who* a Build-A-Bear consumer *could be* beyond our traditional target of kids (especially as the brand became multigenerational, given it had been in business for over twenty years at this juncture). We believed we could drive e-commerce by expanding our base and addressable market to attract tweens, teens, and adults with gifting and collectibles.

We tackled opportunities to renegotiate leases one by one to secure better terms with our mall landlords with shorter time horizons to have more flexibility. We drove down manufacturing costs and diversified our factory base. We reevaluated our licensed relationships and the entire product portfolio with the goal of delivering more business with increased efficiency and expanded margins. And we developed innovative marketing strategies designed to improve our ability to drive more of our *own* Build-A-Bear traffic, given that "organic" mall traffic, which we had historically relied on as a primarily mall-based retailer, was becoming less and less reliable or consistent.

As part of the effort to break through the noise and provide new reasons for consumers to visit our locations, even if they were not planning a regular mall trip, we launched a new National Teddy Bear Day annual event and, a year or so later, developed another new concept to increase consumer trial by leveraging the most popular reason guests first experience the brand—their birthday. The concept was called the Birthday Treat Bear. The idea was to allow the guest to pay the age of the birthday child for the bear during their birthday month. Simple and fun!

This concept provides an incentive for a child's inaugural experience at Build-A-Bear to be at an earlier age than what had been the current average age of a child's first visit. If successful, it could add a year or more to our "lifetime value" calculations. And that could be financially meaningful. We called the idea the "Count Your Candles" program, and we made the offer available to all our loyal Bonus Club members. Another potential benefit of the concept was broadening the socioeconomic accessibility of our brand by having a potentially lower entry-level price point—since it was dependent on the age of the child. Theoretically, the younger the child was on their birthday, the lower the price of the Birthday Treat Bear but the greater potential lifetime value of the guest. It was like a relative acquisition cost.

Next, we needed to come up with a way to introduce this new Birthday Treat Bear to consumers. The idea was to make the opportunity for kids to "pay their age" available to anyone as a special promotion on a single day for a small selection of furry friends.

However, because the year-to-date mall traffic was so tough, and our store sales had been suffering, a week before the event we ran the data to estimate guest turnout using models from a number of large promotions from the past (like National Teddy Bear Day) to assess what would happen if we included *all* of our available products during the in-store-only "Pay Your Age Day" event designed to launch the Birthday Treat Bear. Also, because we were closely managing expenses, we limited the marketing investment to only social media and public relations.

Then, a week later, on a Thursday in July 2018, I was awoken around five o'clock in the morning by my team, some of whom were already at the Bear Quarters. Several of the UK stores were being shut down by mall security due to the crowds generated by the overwhelming reaction to our Pay Your Age Day promotion.

It was difficult to comprehend what they were saying. I quickly searched the internet on my phone to find the unbelievable visuals and news. Lines for Build-A-Bear were snaking through the malls. I got dressed as quickly as possible and drove to BQ to join the team in our boardroom, which had already become a makeshift war room. Many of the functional areas were present around the table. The UK team was on speakerphone. We only had a few hours before the North

American stores were going to open on the East Coast, and lines were already forming at the malls on this side of the Atlantic Ocean. The mood was confused and grim. Out of concern, we started posting social messages for people *not* to come to Build-A-Bear for Pay Your Age Day, but they were lining up anyway.

I am going to pause for a moment and be crystal clear: What was happening and about to happen was literally incomprehensible and impossible to predict. To my knowledge, never has it happened before and not since. It was an especially shocking outcome because it happened during a time of multiple years of continual and unprecedented mall traffic decline.

But on that day, in one of the worst mall traffic years in recent history, in one of the lowest mall traffic months of the year, during a random weekday, it has been estimated that over half a million people lined up to come to Build-A-Bear Workshop locations around the country and across the globe. Lines were even twisting and turning outside into the mall parking lots. Food courts ran out of food. Police were called in to manage the crowds. Press was showing up everywhere.

As we shockingly watched the average estimated wait time turn into *hours*, it became clear that we would not be able to service all the people in line before the end of the business day. We had enough *product*; we just did not have enough *time*.

There was not an easy solution. The entire day, the team stayed in the moment—making choices and providing information in real time to the frontline teams, with the goal of assessing the best decisions possible for our guests, our associates, and the company, while balancing mounds of what seemed like never-ending conflicting information in a situation that felt completely outside the realm of reality, all with the growing pressures of the news and social media. Build-A-Bear's Pay Your Age Day was trending across mulitple social media platforms that day, causing my teenage son to be alarmed enough to call me during work ... for the first time ever.

There is nothing that our dedicated associates dislike more while doing their jobs than disappointing a guest, especially a child. Although I know this was an upsetting situation for many people that day, which never makes any of us happy, I remain in awe and sincerely appreciative as to how the vast majority of our amazing bear builders and our valued guests took it all in stride.

Toward the end of the day, our external public relations group was contacted by a number of media outlets for me to do a live television interview the next morning. We decided that the *Today* show was the best option, given the viewer demographics and strong ratings. This was going to be high pressure.

There was just enough time for me to drive home, pack, and catch the last plane out of St. Louis to New York City. The only time I had to prep for the interview was on the plane, so the PR lead bought a ticket too, and we worked through the strategy at forty thousand feet.

After little sleep, I was on my way to 30 Rock and the NBC studios to meet with Willie Geist and Hoda Kotb for a live *Today* segment. My objective was to share the original goal of the Birthday Treat Bear and how that led to the Pay Your Age Day promotion, apologize that we were not able to service everyone, and assure that our guests understood that we were offering a makeup voucher to use through the rest of the summer. Additionally, I wanted to let people know that the "Count Your Candles" program, which was the impetus for the promo, was still available and would remain a part of our furry friend selection all year round.

Building up to and after the *Today* interview, the press coverage was overwhelming, generating an estimated one billion media impressions in about a twenty-four-hour period.

For an admittedly uncomfortable situation, I have since been informed that my *Today* interview has been used in classrooms and companies as a case study in executive media crisis training. And at the end of the year, *Fortune* did an analysis on CEO apologies during the previous twelve months. The magazine plotted the quality of the CEO apology on a two-by-two chart with "sincere to forced" on the x-axis and "preemptive to overdue" on the y-axis. Build-A-Bear, with comparatively less guidance and resources, was rated the best, based on the apology's combination of "sincere and preemptive." This was compared to a cadre of other well-known companies like Twitter, Facebook, Uber, CBS, Nike, and Starbucks.

Although not for the most flattering of circumstances, I couldn't help but think how extraordinary it was for me and our company to be on this chart with organizations many times our size and with corporate moguls like Mark Zuckerberg and Jack Dorsey. Surely, somehow, this had to somehow be acknowledging the overwhelming consumer awareness and undertapped power of the brand.

By the end of that year, even though Pay Your Age Day became the biggest day ever for plush units sold in Build-A-Bear's history, and the ongoing Count Your Candles Birthday Treat Bear became (and has remained) one of the highest unit-selling products in our line, it was not enough to offset the overwhelming negative financial drag on the company caused by the combination of the fundamental changes in the consumer shopping patterns shifting away from brick-and-mortar retail, particularly in malls, and the Brexit impact. Subsequently, we reported a loss in 2018, which turned out to be the worst financial year we had recorded since I had taken the helm at the company. It was obviously very disheartening for all of us.

Deep inside, however, I still felt our brand power hypothesis and the strategy was right. Again, although never the intent and certainly with no pride in disappointing any of our valued customers, wasn't the Pay Your Age Day experience sort of an accidental proof point that we could be sitting on a megabrand, if we could just figure out a way to monetize the equity?

With diligence and tenacity, by the end of fiscal 2019, the company had returned to profitability following that significant loss in the prior year, which, given that the continued underlying market pressures persisted, was a remarkable accomplishment by the team.

Honestly, we were all very much looking forward to 2020, given that we had worked so hard to complete the prior year with a positive shift in momentum, a solid balance sheet, and a good cash position. We also expected to complete a number of long-term projects in the coming months to improve our omnichannel capabilities, so we could continue to grow our increasingly important e-commerce business. We had some new Build-A-Bear plush offerings from two of the best licenses in the industry sitting in the pipeline: the character eventually named Grogu, from the newly launched *Star Wars* spin-off *The Mandalorian*, which had become a cultural phenom known as "Baby Yoda," was scheduled to be released in the first half of the year, and our first-time collection of the highly requested powerhouse evergreen property *Harry Potter*, which was scheduled for the back half of the year.

At an annual investor conference in January 2020, after we preannounced the expectation of our positive 2019 results, and I unveiled a sample Baby Yoda to the crowd, someone clicked an unauthorized photo, and much to our surprise, the news went viral, causing yet another one-billion-media-impression public relations event for Build-A-Bear.

Because that investor conference caused some growing anticipation around our full earnings release for fiscal 2019, which was scheduled for early March 2020, we made arrangements for me to fly to New York to be interviewed on *Mornings with Maria* with Maria Bartiromo on Fox News, the day after the earnings call.

In preparation, during a Build-A-Bear board of directors meeting, the audit committee had reviewed a draft of the press release, which was scheduled to hit the wire before the market opened on March 11. However, even though we had just announced a nice recovery and were seeing positive momentum with plans to launch some great new licensed products, a wave of concern came over me considering the provision of financial guidance for the upcoming fiscal year.

This thing called "coronavirus" was really starting to ramp up, with big news headlines from the day prior to our board meeting including that four thousand people had died worldwide from coronavirus and that Italy was in lockdown. And now, there was an infected US cruise ship that was not allowed to disembark. We were also aware of the virus from another perspective, having already started to diversify our production plans because some factories in China were in lockdown.

In the eleventh hour, given the increasing uncertainty, we decided to delete our financial expectations for 2020 from the 2019 year-end earnings announcement. And because of the growing travel concerns, we changed the interview on *Mornings with Maria* to be via satellite. On the show, I discussed the year-end results, the launch of Baby Yoda (which, thank goodness, was already "on the water" from China), and our tentative plans and ability to shift to our e-commerce business if stores had to temporarily shut down due to the virus, although it seemed like an incomprehensible concept at the time.

In response to the growing COVID-19 threat, the company quickly devised a plan to split our Bear Quarters team into two weekly shifts, with cleaning crews scheduled to come in on the weekends. I was in shift B, with our CFO in shift A, to keep us separated, just in case things continued to escalate.

As such, he went into the office the following week, and I worked from home. Our IT team kicked into high gear to get everyone ready for remote work as quickly as possible. But shift B—including me—never stepped back in the office for regular work, and by mid-March, we had done the unthinkable.

We had completely shuttered our corporate offices, our call center, and then, within a forty-eight-hour period, all of the stores in our entire corporately managed retail operations across multiple countries. This forced action led to furloughing over 90 percent of our workforce—a really difficult decision to make for a company with heart.

Like so many, we had no idea what was next, for ourselves, our families, the economy, or our company. We had instituted a morning conference call with an extended leadership team—every day at 8:00 a.m. central time, weekends included—and put together a process for making decisions efficiently and effectively cascading information quickly. Everything was moving so fast that choices had to be made in real time with imperfect information. We were in crisis mode.

There are lots of critical elements to consider for impactful crisis management, not the least of which is recognizing *when* you are in a crisis. Once you have embraced that fact, it is important to understand that you must manage differently than before.

Even when there are critical outcomes on the line, change can still be difficult for people and teams. Habit is strong. New rules of engagement needed to be explained and consistently enforced.

I knew I would have to update my approach and leadership style. First, every decision needed to be about what was right in front of us. This is counterintuitive for well-run and effective management teams. Most of the time, the best teams weigh all sorts of pros and cons of big decisions and directives, balancing the short- and long-term outcomes. But in a crisis, it's time to make the best decision in the "now" and worry about the later, well, *later*, because you are simply trying to assure that there is a later to worry about.

Second, the leadership team and I had to become much more dictatorial in an environment where we had a culture cultivated to be more collaborative. Often in these situations, fear can freeze companies and decision makers. However, expert advice leans toward the idea that it is better to *do something*. Although a "wait and see" management style can work under certain situations, an emergency is generally not one of them.

Once we had shifted into full business crisis mode, we started immediately assessing: "What do we have?" and "What can we do?"

Well, we had some cash, because what now had become a pandemic hit at a point in time after our two biggest holiday seasons, Christmas and Valentine's Day. We had just flipped the switch on a new warehouse management system in February, which was going to allow us to manage our e-commerce business in new and more efficient ways. As long as we could safely operate the Ohio-based warehouse and fulfillment center, we could keep our online business running. And because we weren't shipping to stores that were forced to close due to local and governmental mandates, we had plenty of inventory in the warehouse to sell online. Therefore, even if the factories stayed closed for an extended period of time, we could continue to generate sales and preserve cash, at least for a while.

Once again, we were surrounded by companies filing for bankruptcy, and by early April our stock was trading around one dollar a share, ushering in the reality that we, too, were being priced by the investment community as if we were doomed.

The level of pressure and details to work through in a situation like this are difficult to describe and impossible to list. Some of my mentors and bosses from the past reached out to see how we were doing and offered encouragement and some amazing advice. One of those people was Matt Rubel. He talked me through his take on the crisis and sent me an article, which was technically about the recession, but there was one passage that really intrigued me: "What if this recession (replace "recession" with "COVID-19 crisis") was the luckiest thing that ever happened to my business?"[23]

Note: This question is meant to be an existential postulation, not a literal one. It is not the intent of this discussion to imply that COVID-19 was *lucky* or *good* in any way, for anybody. People suffered and died, and continue to do so. It is simply an exercise in contemplating the purposeful exploration of the value created by a shift in perspective, even in difficult situations. Sometimes you can only get to the right answer if you are willing to ask the right question.

As we tried to change our point of view, our responses began to change from "What are we going to do to keep from going out of business?" to "Wow, what are we going to do with all this 'free time' when we don't have to worry about operating our stores for once?"

It's a little mind blowing, but just the thought of this idea gave us a lot of clarity, a lot of hope, and a lot of energy—and fast.

The first thing I did with this perspective shift may sound odd and seemingly meaningless, but it was critical. I renamed our daily morning executive remote gatherings. No longer would they be known as the "COVID crisis meetings." They would be called "success meetings," and we began *acting as if* we were not only going to survive, but we were going to thrive.

Back on March 10, 2020, we had removed our financial guidance from our earnings press release due to the unknown threat of a looming

---

23   Mark Payne, "Innovating for a Recession," Fahrenheit 212, 2020, https://www.fahrenheit-212.com/boiling-point/innovating-for-recession.

global pandemic, which ushered in one of the most difficult times in modern history and the history of Build-A-Bear Workshop.

One year and one day later, on March 11, 2021, the company announced its 2020 year-end and fourth-quarter results. Build-A-Bear's pretax income had far exceeded expectations with an increase of nearly 21 percent versus the prior year's fourth quarter. We achieved triple-digit e-commerce growth for both the quarter and the year. We had reopened the vast majority of our retail stores after rewriting the service manuals and retraining our teams to translate our "high-touch" retail model that we were famous for into "high-experience" with "no touch," at least six feet apart. With the reopening of our locations, we were able to bring back the majority of the support staff at BQ as well, albeit in an ongoing remote work environment.

The company ended the year with more cash than it had at the end of the prior year (before the beginning of the pandemic) and with no borrowings on the credit facility—despite the complete shutdown of the number one revenue-generating arm, the retail stores, during a meaningful portion of the year.

Finally, the team had somehow actually leveraged the situation as a moment to reorganize the company and accelerate the execution of a number of initiatives that had otherwise been planned well into the future—leapfrogging our strategic objectives by many months across a variety of functional areas, especially regarding our digital transformation.

MarketWatch's headline the morning of our 2020 year-end release read, "Build-A-Bear Shares Soar After Earnings Blow Past Expectations." The stock price closed that day at $8.75, a 20 percent increase from the opening price and over eight times the price at the pandemic low.

This was followed a few months later with the celebration of the "making" of the company's two hundred millionth furry friend. We had saved the company, and we had done it with heart.

 A Question from the Heart

DO YOU KNOW WHEN TRIUMPH OVER TRIAL IS LESS ABOUT SKILL OR TENACITY AND MORE ABOUT TRUST?

Nikola Tesla once said, "Instinct is something which transcends knowledge." Well, in a situation where there is no direct knowledge to reference, you have no choice but to recognize that during some trials in life, you must *trust your instincts.*

As Malcolm Gladwell notes in his thought-provoking book *Blink: The Power of Thinking Without Thinking,* ideas, insights, and direction don't always come from spreadsheets, research, and long contemplation. "There can be as much value in the blink of an eye as in months of rational analysis," he wrote.

Sometimes we are capable of taking a small amount of data—a "thin slice," as Gladwell likes to call it—to draw conclusions using a combination of experience and intuition.

Many of us recognize when an athlete is "in the zone." After years of training, in the crunch moments they are prepared to instinctually operate at a high level. They do not need to stop and analyze the situation before making the basket, shooting the goal, throwing the touchdown pass, or hitting the home run. In fact, if they stopped to analyze the situation, the moment would be lost during the act of "thinking."

"Blink" is the businessperson's version of being "in the zone." But unlike an athlete, where the time pressure to make the decision is often obvious—the clock is ticking, the game is tied—the businessperson may not always recognize the criticality of the situation.

236

Credit to the team, in both the Pay Your Age Day promotion and the COVID-19 crisis, we had an understanding, in the moment, that these were make-or-break, corporate-history-making situations.

In both circumstances, it was important to realize that my rapid-fire thoughts and directions concerning what we needed to do next were not merely guesses, even though they were not made with the traditional collaborative discussions, data analysis, and rigor, which, admittedly, can be uncomfortable for someone who is known to stop a meeting and demand of the team: "Do the math!"

But without the benefit of time, I was forced to quickly dig through the files of experience in my head and instinctually connect dots to create informed answers in an environment where we did not have a moment to waste. And for the most part, based on the outcome, the right decisions were made by both me and the leadership team.

I have often told my teams through the years that a good idea, executed with excellence, is many times more powerful than an excellent idea executed poorly. Don't over*think*—over*execute*. But this was extreme.

What I have come to realize is that, as you grow and learn, the ability to trust your instincts is not a luxury but a necessity, and not just in a crisis situation. The faster your business moves or the bigger your business oversight becomes, the more decisions you will be tasked to make quickly in uncertainty and with imperfect information.

Indeed, at some point when you have accumulated enough experience and information, learning to trust your "blink" instincts is the last critical step to cracking the code to reach your goals.

This is not suggesting that you can or should run a business or live your life entirely by shooting from the hip. Using data and information is critical—but you can't let it use you. Recognize when your cumulative history of experiences, successes, failures, and knowledge may have given you an ability, or even an edge, to do more than just make lucky guesses. At some point, it starts to come together and becomes second nature. One sign that you may be "in the zone" is when you begin to see patterns and recognize trends before they are obvious.

A book by Columbia Business School professor Rita McGrath, *Seeing Around Corners*, addresses the importance of this ability for leaders by referring to the initial turnaround approach at Build-A-Bear as a case study. She specifically notes that good leaders learn how to spot "inflection points in business before they happen."

Despite how "good" at this idea I may have been at that point, the COVID-19 crisis became an unwelcome master class in the art of listening to and trusting my instincts.

Now, Create *Your* Story: Listen to Your Instincts

Ultimately, if you are afraid of making decisions in uncertainty, you're likely going to be very uncomfortable in a leadership position. However, with enough experience and tribulation, you will eventually start to feel like you *know* the answer because your brain, your gut, your whatever has already figured it out before you have had time to think about it. How is that possible? Well, you may not be able to pinpoint all the data that you are instinctually sourcing, but it is real. You don't panic. In fact, somehow, you may start to find that the more acute the situation, the calmer you become. You have been through the trials, so in the crisis, you *instinctually* trust your ability to quickly identify the right next step.

I know it seems like I have spent a whole lot of time and effort in this book to share new ways for you to "think." And now, at the very end, I am telling you that the real secret to success is to "stop thinking." But it is not that easy. Even if you have the experience to lean on, even if you have been through the gauntlet, you can't follow your instincts until you can hear what they are trying to tell you.

The problem is that instincts often do not yell and scream. They whisper. If your world, your mind, your life is too loud, they will be drowned out. You have to *learn* to be quiet and *listen* to them first.

In April 2019, after what seemed like a constant barrage of challenges in the business, I decided to take a short trip to Arizona by myself to simply relax and recharge. I quickly surfed the internet to find what looked like a nice spa option. I was anticipating just being alone for a few days, eating organic food, doing a little yoga, getting a massage, and sitting by the pool with a glass of wine, watching the sunset over the gorgeous red rocks of Sedona. I had also planned to take a class on getting centered, which sounded like something I would enjoy.

> You can't follow your instincts until you can hear what they are trying to tell you.

After the white van picked me up from the Phoenix airport, we headed off for the nearly two-hour ride to Sedona. Then, we turned off the paved road and started to rumble through the rust-colored landscape for nearly fifteen minutes with the dust billowing behind us. I did not know exactly what was happening. I didn't realize this resort was so far off the beaten path. I even had a fleeting thought that maybe I was being kidnapped—*naaay*, but seriously, where was this place?

When I arrived, there was no masseuse with whom to schedule a relaxing rubdown, and no bartender to pour a nice chardonnay. This was not a pampering resort and spa. The facilities were unusually sparse, with concrete floors and no amenities—not even a hair dryer—plus there were signs everywhere for attendees to remain quiet.

In my online haste, I had unwittingly secured reservations at a genuine Taoist center.

By *Taoism*, I am not referring so much to what would be regarded as the religion, per se, but to the general philosophy of learning to live in harmony. In harmony with yourself, with others, and with the universe. Although somewhat confusing and maybe even upsetting to those who have grown up with the sensibilities of the Western world, it is the admittance and acceptance that we are all connected and we are really never in control of anything in our lives except ourselves, even when we think we are.

The fact that I learned about the fundamentals of Taoism by "accidentally" stumbling into a Taoist center for well-being, just months before the most unprecedented global economic and health crisis in our lifetimes, is a pretty crazy coincidence—or was it "planned serendipity"?

Either way, having the experience of being "in the zone" requires you to learn to listen to your instincts. And I have learned that one way to be quiet enough to hear them is the *M* word—yes, *meditation*.

Before you throw down the book and walk away, remember this is Short Fuse talking here! All I am asking you to do is be still and quiet and breathe and try not to think of anything for just a little while every day. No candles, no "oms," no crossed legs, no nothing. In fact, doing (and thinking) nothing is entirely the point.

If you need some scientific proof of the potential positive impact on your life, there is tons of it. Will the Mayo Clinic suffice? In a recent online article called "Meditation: A Simple, Fast Way to Reduce Stress," the famed clinic staff outlined numerous benefits to the practice, ranging from gaining a new perspective on stressful situations to reducing and managing symptoms for various health conditions such as tension headaches, sleep problems, anxiety, depression, and high blood pressure.[24]

Let's try it for five or ten minutes. Get comfortable and close your eyes. Take a deep breath, hold it for three counts, and then breathe out slowly. Do this three times. Sit quietly and try to think of nothing. When your mind intervenes, just acknowledge the thoughts and go back to thinking nothing. When you are finished, write what pops into your mind on the attached page. These thoughts may be some clues to what your instincts are trying to tell you.

If you are not ready for the *M* word, find your own way to calm your mind. Some people run or sit outside or walk in nature or even enjoy a regular massage. The key is not what you are doing but what you are (or, more importantly, are *not*) thinking. Yoga is another common approach to helping you focus and calm your mind as well. Whatever you choose to do, allow your mind to relax a little while every day. Early mornings are best—*before* you check the news or your email—because you can squeeze it in before your crazy brain gets all revved up worrying about the day and everything that you need to do. Don't worry, all of that will still be there after you are finished.

---

24   "Meditation: A Simple, Fast Way to Reduce Stress," Mayo Clinic, April 22, 2020, https://www.mayoclinic.org/tests-procedures/meditation/in-depth/meditation/art-20045858.

LISTEN TO YOUR INSTINCTS

LISTEN TO YOUR INSTINCTS

CALM YOUR MIND FOR FIVE TO TEN MINUTES. BREATHE AND FOCUS ON NOTHING. WHEN YOU'RE FINISHED, WRITE WHAT POPS INTO YOUR MIND HERE:

But Wait, There's More

My hometown is only a couple of hours from some of the best rapids in the country on a river called the Ocoee, just north of Chattanooga, Tennessee. Some of these rapids, which are pouring out of the Appalachian Mountains, have a high level of difficulty, with at least one of the runs being used for the canoe event during the 1996 Atlanta Summer Olympics. During high school, some friends and I decided to go white water rafting on the Ocoee.

In preparation for the raft ride, we went through a morning training session. We were taught how to use a paddle and outfitted in life jackets with extra head support floats and helmets. While geared up we practiced paddling together and following various commands of the trip leader. We were counseled on what to do if (or rather, when) we were thrown from the raft, which included putting your feet downriver and just going with the flow. We were told that no matter what happens, just stay calm because we will all end up in the same place in the end.

I have often used the analogy of white water rafting in comparison to running a business with my organization. We are a team. We are in the boat together. We need to paddle in unison with the same goal in mind. We need to understand who is the "trip leader." We need to stay calm in the rough rapids.

But when I signed a deal with ForbesBooks in January of 2020, there was no way to know that Olympic-caliber rapids were lurking just around the river bend, and that the "ending" would be nothing like the one I had planned, no matter how hard I paddled.

I wrote this book in my spare time during a year when the world was in COVID-19 lockdown. It was a surprisingly grounding and cathartic process. However, when it came time to complete the final chapter, I struggled. I felt like there had not been enough time to absorb or reflect on the recent rough water.

As I completed the first draft on Memorial Day 2021, it dawned on me that this is the morning that my dad shared the news about my grandmother's death all those years ago, which ultimately spurred me to climb that massive beech tree.

This reflection caused me to realize that during the course of writing these thirteen stories, I had begun to believe that maybe life is a little less like a beech tree and a little more like the Ocoee River.

Early on we are taught to fight to make the climb, reach the new height, or achieve the next goal. Having dreams and plans and achievements are a part of life, but maybe it doesn't have to be a constant struggle—other than the fact that it may be a necessary part of the human experience before we're able to just get in the raft and enjoy the ride on the river.

Ironically, even in the raft, we often still try to create the illusion that we are in control, by paddling, yelling instructions, or leaning left or right to avoid the rapids. But we are not in control. Did you know that during the most difficult white water, you are instructed to stop paddling? In fact, they specifically tell you to pull in the oars and let the river do the work.

In 2020, with no sense of confusion or defeat, I decided to stop frantically paddling against the raging white water and I threw my oars out of the boat. And guess what? I ended up exactly where I was supposed to be, actually in a place far better than I had ever envisioned, at exactly the right moment.

When you can appreciate this beautiful dichotomy, then you have really started to learn the art of trial and trust and how to enjoy our fascinating dance with the universe.

With practice, that can lead to unlocking the power of your personal experiences to create a life you love, filled with stories and heart.

WITH GRATITUDE FROM THE BOTTOM OF MY HEART

One Mother's Day a few years ago, my youngest daughter, who was about four at the time, gave me a small present that she had adorably wrapped in many layers of crumpled paper. I could not imagine what she had placed in this apparently very important package. I glanced at Russ to get any clue, but he shrugged in a manner as if to say, "No idea."

What could this be? Maybe a Play-Doh creation, a plastic ring, a folded-up coloring page? Whatever it was, as I continued to carefully unwrap the gift, layer after layer, I was preparing to react with some over-the-top mommy gratefulness and awe. Underneath the final overly taped tissue paper, I discovered a small white box. I slowly removed the lid and found *nothing*. It was completely empty. I looked curiously at her big, proud brown eyes as she smiled from ear to ear and proclaimed, "Momma, it's a box of *love!*"

And with that, this small empty box became one of the best gifts I have ever received.

It's that simple. We see what we want to see. We decide the meaning of things and events. And the meaning we give them influences and impacts our lives and our futures.

Some say that when we finally "get it," we can look inside the gift box of life and see the good in everything and be *grateful* for it *all*.

What? Be grateful for it all? For everyone and everything, the good and the bad?

That is a tall order for most, so a good way to start is by just *acknowledging* it all and at least appreciating the contrast, because without the bad, how would you know what the good feels like?

However, even to do this effectively, it is widely believed that you have to let go of hate, resentment, and regret from the past. That does not change the fact that this process remains an important part of being able to become the best *you* you can be. Some of you may be thinking that I have no right to suggest something like this to you. You might think, *She doesn't know my story*, or *She hasn't been through what I've been through*, and you'd most likely be right. Yes, even though I have had occasional trials climbing my chosen life tree, among other things, I was fortunate enough to be born in a developed country to loving parents at a time in history where little girls' lives were not mostly predestined.

If you still believe that it is not possible for you to "let it all go," consider that a man who had every right to have looked back on his life and his adversaries with anger and distain once said, "Resentment is like drinking poison and then hoping it will kill your enemies"— Nelson Mandela knew how to redefine the events in his life to serve a purpose. Not only that; he outlined in his 1994 inaugural speech that "it is our light, not our darkness, that most frightens us." Deciding to release hate and be grateful is one sure way to let your light shine.

You may have heard the saying, "Today is a gift; that's why it is called *the present*." Well, every day we receive and decide what is in our own little gift box—our present. Each day, we can look inside and see bad things from the past, or all the terrible things that someone said about us, or all the awful things we can imagine that are sure to happen in our future.

Or not.

What's inside the present? You decide. Just like I decided that my "empty" Mother's Day gift box was filled with love.

For me, this *present* moment is filled with appreciation. I acknowledge it all. For without it *all*, this book would not exist.

From my parents and hometown that gave me the roots that I sometimes felt were holding me back, only to find they were grounding me to be able to grow high in the sky; to my teachers, bosses, and mentors who pushed me to try harder, gave me a chance, or believed in me when I could not; to my friends and colleagues who have been there through thick and thin with honest reflection and encouraging words; to my husband and children who provide a loving source of stability and joy; to the difficult people, heartbreaks, gut-wrenching disappointments, and angering challenges; and to my current Build-A-Bear family

> Deciding to release hate and be grateful is one sure way to let your light shine.

and wonderful team who never cease to amaze me with their drive and passion to "add a little more heart to life"—I thank you.

And finally, I am grateful to the team at Forbes that came together to almost *make* me write this book, no matter what I did or said or the many reasons I could find not to write it.

Create Your Own Story

This final exercise is one that many of us have been taught since we were children. The wisdom embedded in the concept of "counting your blessings" is still so powerful and yet so simple that it is hard to truly appreciate. Some of the scientifically proven benefits of gratefulness, highlighted in a range of *Forbes* articles citing numerous studies, include the following:

- Healthier relationships

- Improved physical health

- Enhanced psychological health

- Reduced aggression

- Better sleep

- More self-esteem

- Increased mental strength

Wow. Gratefulness sounds like a wonder drug, except it's free and all the side effects are good! If these potential positive results aren't keys to success and living a life you love, I don't know what else could be.

Although there are a lot of wonderful ways to increase your gratefulness, one is to get involved with a philanthropic or charitable organization. I am sure your time, talent, and/or treasure would be welcomed by those in need, and it is never a bad thing for you to be reminded of how fortunate you likely already are. Even one day of volunteering with the goal of aiding someone in a disadvantaged situation or helping toward the achievement of an objective for the greater good can be a blessed and transformational experience. My parents happened to have fostered this idea in me at an early age, but it's never too late to make this choice.

Another way is to practice the "art" of gratefulness on a regular basis. I have included a place for you to start a gratefulness file. Simply begin by making a list of the things and people in your life that you are thankful for—review it and add to it often. Just this process alone, when combined with an open heart, is well documented to positively impact your life.

With that, it seems appropriate to *thank you* for taking the time to read this book. I hope you enjoy the continuous process of unlocking the power of your personal stories to create a life you love! Please share the stories you are creating in your life at storiesandheart@buildabear.com.

GRATEFULNESS FILE

Here's an easy way to start your Gratefulness File. List whatever blessings there are in your life. It's sometimes easier to think about it categorically as outlined below. I fashioned this after my grandmother's old recipe file box, as I believe this is a recipe for happiness.

Get down in the details. Are you grateful you can breathe without thinking about it? Are you happy you have fingers, eyes, a heart? Do you have access to food and clean water? Can you read and write? Are there people in your life who love you? Did you sleep in a warm bed last night? Did the sun rise this morning? Once you get started, it should be powerful and overwhelming how much good is in your life.

FAMILY & FRIENDS

HEALTH & LIFE

HOME

NATURE

EPILOGUE

Even though we emerged from 2020 intact and with some momentum, as we kicked off 2021 we still had to dig out of a deep hole. To change the mindset of the organization, we introduced a new core value to the list of inspirational words, like *collaborate* and *learn*, that had not changed since 1997. Our new word was *win*, and we renamed the year "202w1n," which was repeated in practically every meeting and update.

Toward the end of 2021, Build-A-Bear was again invited to the New York Stock Exchange for the ninety-eighth anniversary of the Wall Street Christmas Tree Lighting Ceremony. On that day in early December, I was escorted across the floor of the venerated NYSE trading floor to ring the closing bell along with a number of others gathered to celebrate this annual event. The group included the head of the NYSE, leaders of philanthropic organizations, a member of the US Marines, a representative of the Harlem Globe Trotters, two huge costumed character bears, a Christmas Elf, and Santa Claus. The Build-A-Bear PR team had planned for me to be holding one of our teddy bears with a tiny logo T-shirt, but as we were finding our places on the podium, I realized I had forgotten the bear in all of the rush and excitement!

I was disappointed with myself for forgetting the one thing I was supposed to remember to take up on the famous New York Stock Exchange podium, and then I had a crazy idea. As I looked over the balcony, I searched for our CFO in the cheering crowd below and yelled down to him, "Throw me a bear!"

The countdown for ringing the closing bell had already begun as he quickly scanned the trading floor for one of our branded bears we had handed out to the crowd earlier. He secured a teddy and lurched back through the throng of people as the count continued—and then, almost like magic (and as I recall, maybe even in slow motion) a teddy bear floated up through the air on national television right into my hands, just in time for the gavel to come down and end the trading day. And what a trading day it was!

Holding the teddy bear, standing next to Santa, I waved and clapped with the bell clanging and the crowd cheering. That same morning during our earnings call we had shared record-breaking results both for the third quarter of 2021 and for the year to date. We also announced a special dividend, a stock buyback program, and the raising of our annual guidance for both revenue and profit, which would lead to one of the best years in the history of the company. In fact, 2021 eventually became the most profitable year in Build-A-Bear's nearly twenty-five years of existence.

That morning, BBW's stock price jumped to over twenty dollars per share upon the news, hitting a ten-year high. *The Street* reported BBW as one of the top five stock gainers for the day, noting that the shares had "skyrocketed" with a 27 percent increase. This is on top of *Newsweek* having already named BBW as a top-twenty-five stock for the year only a few weeks before.

After weeks of script writing and preparation, here is part of my opening remarks on the call: "Since 1997, Build-A-Bear has grown from a single retail location in the St. Louis Galleria Mall to an evolved and diversified global corporation reflecting many market and consumer changes. Most of the business model evolution has taken place in the last eight years since I took the helm in 2013, with this passionate team staying focused on successfully turning around a company that had endured eight consecutive years of comparable stores' sales declines by 2012, into today's thriving entity that is now poised for a compelling future."

After having just caught that teddy bear up on the podium at the NYSE, adding another storied moment to my life, I was reminded that the key word from my opening remarks was *team*. Even as I was afforded an opportunity to stand at arguably the epicenter of the business world—at the moment it really mattered—in a last-minute effort, on a crazy whim, the CFO of the company went out of his way to quickly locate and throw me a bear. In a heartbeat, he had instinctually gone the extra mile to create an unforgettably great moment to end the day on a perfect note, even though I had made a mistake. That is what amazing teams and teammates do. And that is what the heart-filled people do at Build-A-Bear every day. No matter what, we work together to try to find a way for everybody to get a teddy bear when they really need one. Again, we had focused on an aspirational goal and came together as a team. As someone told me later, "Sharon, we TWENTY-TWENTY-*WON*!"

But Wait, There's More

After the bell finished clanging, Santa turned to me and said, "Great catch!" Then he paused for just a moment and, almost unbelievably, asked me with eerie seriousness, "What can I bring you for Christmas this year?"

I responded, "Santa, I can't think of a thing."

He gave me a warm smile, and together with my teddy bear, we left the New York Stock Exchange podium and headed toward the Christmas tree lighting on Wall Street.

ABOUT THE AUTHOR

Since 2013, Sharon Price John has served as the president and CEO of Build-A-Bear Workshop, Inc. In her tenure as CEO of the publicly traded company (NYSE: BBW), she has overseen a return to profitability, the diversification of the business that included embracing a digital transformation, and the revitalization and consumer expansion of the nearly twenty-five-year-old brand to create a springboard for years to come. But, before she was included in the small group of women who lead companies traded on the New York Stock Exchange, before serving as a change agent for multiple brands and business units at Fortune 500 companies, and before working in New York City and attending Columbia University, Sharon was just a small-town girl in Tennessee with big dreams.

After graduating from the University of Tennessee, Sharon got her first big break in Manhattan working for DDB/Needham Worldwide, a top advertising agency, and was eventually recruited to another large agency where she became the account supervisor on the M&M/Mars account.

Sharon would later go on to earn her MBA at Columbia University, after which she began her toy career at Mattel in an entry-level position on the Barbie brand. She spent five years working her way up to vice president there and eventually moved back East to work for another toy company, Hasbro. Seven years later, after helping to revitalize brands like Nerf and Littlest Pet Shop, Sharon was ready for her next challenge and was tapped to be the president of the Stride Rite Children's Group (SRCG). Within a couple of years of her taking the helm, SRGC had returned to profitability and was named Company of the Year by *Earnshaw's* magazine.

Sharon caught the attention of Build-A-Bear Workshop in 2013 and was recruited to St. Louis to take the helm from the legendary founder, Maxine Clark. Sharon was placed in charge of a company that was still struggling to recover from the Great Recession and faced a number of challenges as consumer shopping habits shifted from traditional retail to e-commerce.

For nearly a decade Sharon has guided the beloved brand and company through some of the most tumultuous times in business history by successfully navigating the "retail apocalypse," Brexit, and a global pandemic that forced the company to close all of its retail stores in 2020. During this evolutionary time, she was featured in the hit TV show *Undercover Boss*; unveiled the Build-A-Bear "Baby Yoda" at an investor conference that went viral, generating over one billion media impressions; and was at the helm during the now (in)famous "Pay Your Age Day" promotion that flooded the national news as an estimated half a million people lined up at malls across North America and Europe on a single day to make a furry friend.

Even during this time of challenge and change, she and her team simultaneously worked to strategically reorganize, rebuild the company's digital infrastructure, and reposition the brand for the future, which has contributed to fiscal 2021 being the most profitable year in corporate history.

Sharon is a member of the board of directors for Jack in the Box (NASDAQ: JACK), has been named one of the University of Tennessee's top one hundred distinguished alumni of the last one hundred years, and has received alumni recognition from Columbia Women in Business. Sharon is also engaged with a number of philanthropic and business organizations, including being a member of the executive committee for the Toy Industry Association (TIA), serving on the board of KABOOM!, and being a member of The Committee of 200 (C200). Sharon has three children and lives with her husband in St. Louis, Missouri.